Don't Forget the Soap

And Other Reminders from My Fabulous Filipina Mother

Don't Forget the Soap

And Other Reminders from
My Fabulous Filipina Mother

Marie Claire Lim Moore

CANLINK
New York

Published by CANLINK, 1400 Fifth Avenue
Suite 5D, New York, NY 10026

Library of Congress Cataloging-in-Publication Data
Lim Moore, Marie Claire.
Don't Forget the Soap (and other reminders from My Fabulous Filipina Mother) /
Marie Claire Lim Moore – 1st ed.
p.   cm.

ISBN°13 978–0–9898534–1–5
ISBN°10 978–0–9898534–1–1

PRINTED IN THE UNITED STATES OF AMERICA

Editor: Vicky Anastacio
Book design and layout: Nonie Cartagena-dono
Prints: Lenore RS Lim
pp. 6, 14, 71, 195

First paperback edition, 2013

(Detail, frontispiece) Lenore RS Lim: *My Mother's Veil (Ella)*, Computer generated design, 44" x 104", 2010

For my parents, Jose and Lenore,
Alex, Justin, Carlos and Isabel

Contents

Acknowledgements

As a freshman at Yale, I noticed that my roommate would spend a long time reading the "Acknowledgements" page of any book she picked up. I usually skimmed over or even skipped this part so I was intrigued by what was so interesting about this section. One day I asked her and she said, "I like knowing who inspired the book and helped get it published." This has crossed my mind several times as I worked on this project.

I have to start by thanking my immediate family. For everything really but especially for letting this book be the center of dinner conversations and long distance phone calls for the past year. My husband, Alex, for embracing all things Filipino and showering me with more ideas and affection than I ever thought possible. We joke about him having a bad memory but interestingly enough he seems to recall every Raquel-Santos / Lim family story we've ever told (and there are boatloads of them). My mother, Lenore RS Lim, for being the mother, wife, artist, teacher and community leader who inspired this book. My brother, Justin, for helping me recollect childhood stories and, of course, pointing out when I need to take things "one notch down." My two little loves, Carlos and Isabel. If I didn't spend so much time thinking about what kind of people I hope they grow up to be, I probably never would have reflected enough on life to do this.

Special thanks to my father, Jose Lim, who plays a bigger role in this book (and in my life) than the title suggests. As people read the following pages, it will be obvious that I learned as much from my father as I did from my mother, but I want it to be known even to those who don't make it past skimming the acknowledgements.

I am also grateful to my very busy extended family and friends who generously lent their eyes and ears throughout this process: Clorinda Moore, Natasha Muslih, Angelica Kristen Jongco, Tanya Loh, Alexis Neophytides, Julie Barry and Sandhya Devanathan. I am extremely appreciative of the examples set by Carissa Villacorta and Christine Amour-Levar which roused in me the discipline to follow through on this endeavor.

Deepest gratitude to Vicky Anastacio for her patience and time while being the gatekeeper of good grammar. Finally, my heartfelt thanks to Nonie Cartagena-dono for his beautiful work and excellent taste in designing every last inch of this book.

Lenore RS Lim
Orchids 3
Monotype
22.5" x 15"
2008

INTRODUCTION

I'm a second generation Filipina-Canadian-American, which means that while I never personally uprooted my life from the Philippines, I certainly had what my brother and I refer to as "the immigrant experience." It consisted of the following:

- hand me down clothes—actually, hand me down everything
- knock off Barbies (the plastic version where the knees didn't bend)
- relatives staying with us for weeks (or months) at a time
- our family staying with relatives for weeks (or months) at a time
- sponsoring *Lolo* and *Lola* who would live with us[1]
- never traveling light—the *balikbayan* box[2] would often be our second piece of luggage
- canned foods prepared gourmet style
- McDonalds as a special meal out
- "extending" food and beverages (e.g., one packet of Swiss Miss would make 2–3 cups of hot chocolate)
- never throwing anything out (someone in the Philippines could use that)

[1] In Tagalog *Lolo* means "grandfather" and *Lola* means "grandmother."

[2] A *balikbayan* box (literally, "Repatriate box") is a corrugated box containing items sent by an overseas Filipino known as *"balikbayan."*

I love recounting these "immigrant experiences" with my fellow second generation cousins and friends. We can spend hours talking about Spam or the Libby's Corned Beef "key"[3] or reminiscing on how we would all fit into one car. These stories make us appreciate what we have today. Most of us are now married and with our own families. Our kids are used to eating out at least a couple of times a week, they often get the latest toy gadgets before they know they want them and vacation hotels are standard fare.

My husband and I have a two-year-old son and a newborn daughter. Often I find myself wondering how we'll ever instill this appreciation into our kids when they're going to grow up with everything we have today. But I'm intent on trying anyway, starting with myself. I have to admit that every now and then I need some reminders to help keep me in check. I live in an expat bubble full of beautiful people and fabulous things. Day-to-day life here in Singapore revolves around social clubs, overseas travel and the kind of high-end shopping which, to my husband's delight, I can't even bring myself to partake. (Who knew that at a certain price point, you end up saving money?)

For the last several years I've had the opportunity to work in different global cities and experience a life I know I'm so fortunate to have. It's hard not to get caught up in the lifestyle even a little bit so I'm very grateful to have reminders from my mother to help me keep life balanced. These are stories I try to bear in mind whenever I catch my feet floating off the ground (or whenever my brother or husband calls me out on sounding ungrateful, out of touch or just plain over the top). I've been making mental notes of these anecdotes for years now and planning to one day put them in writing so they can be captured properly. I know I won't be the only one who benefits.

I've lost count of the number of people I've seen over the course of my life befriend my mother and look to her for advice on everything from dating to marriage to raising kids to exhibiting

---

[3] The Libby's Corned Beef cans came with a silver metal key on the side so it could be opened even without a can opener.

art to fundraising to party planning. On paper you wouldn't think of her as your big personality or counseling type. She was the shy and soft spoken girl born and raised in Manila and educated by nuns from elementary school until she started college. She describes herself as a late bloomer who didn't fully blossom until 40 and that's probably not much of an exaggeration. The entire time, however, she must have been developing strength behind her convictions and empathy for others before anything else. I'm not sure exactly how she does it, but she manages to reconcile seemingly contradictory qualities and beliefs. One day she is being ordained as an Extraordinary Minister of Holy Communion[4] and the next she is helping a transgender friend make peace with family members.

While there are many sides to my mother her advice and philosophy are always quite simple: *Don't take anything for granted. Not all the experiences you're blessed with. Not your ability to make a difference in a small way. Not each person who helped you along the way.* As I draft these pages, I often think about what kind of book this will be. More than anything, it's a collection of anecdotes that serve to remind me of the values and perspective I want to pass along to my children regardless of any success achieved. These are the story form answers to questions I've been hearing people ask my mother for as long as I can remember. I do offer some practical tips based on mental notes I've made watching her successfully navigate through life balancing home, career, friendships and community. That said, it's not meant to be a prescriptive guide by any means. As should be the case whenever you get advice from a friend, you take away a different perspective and use what works for you.

A few things you'll probably pick up as you read along so I'll go ahead and put them out there now:

1. My family is pretty corny. We've been called the Filipino

---

[4] It sounds extremely fancy, I know, but it just refers to lay people (anybody who is not a deacon, priest or bishop) who give out Communion.

Cleavers, the Filipino Huxtables, you name it and there's no denying it.[5] Growing up we were a walking family sitcom complete with life lessons at the end of each day. Our lunch bags included notes from Mom that said, "Have a nice day," we had jam sessions on a regular basis (Dad on the guitar, Justin on the violin and I on the piano), and we sang all the time in the car (mostly to practice our harmonies for the karaoke session waiting when we got home). All that's been missing is a laugh track.

2. I put my mother on a pedestal. It is, after all, the premise behind this book. Sure, she has her pain points like everyone else (she's kind of a nervous Nellie,[6] she's not the most flexible and she can be overly critical about the "proper" way of doing things) but when it comes to what defines you as a person and your time in this world, no one has a better outlook than my mother and for this reason I hold her in the highest regard.

3. I'm a little old fashioned. I used to joke that my mom and dad were parents of the '50s raising children in the '80s but it turns out I'm a parent of the '80s raising children in the 2010s. What can I say? I like the shared family phone, I still believe in old rules, e.g., girls don't call boys, and the thought of young teens watching certain scenes from *Glee* and *Gossip Girl* makes me cringe.[7] Can't they save one person's virginity so all the kids not having sex in

---

[5] References to *Leave it to Beaver* and *The Cosby Show*. While very different television shows (the first featuring the idealized suburban family in the '50s and '60s and the second an upper middle-class African-American family in Brooklyn, NY in the '80s and '90s) both exemplified the traditional ideal family.

[6] Term used to describe someone who is always worrying unnecessarily.

[7] *Glee* and *Gossip Girl* are contemporary American teen drama television series.

high school have someone left to relate to? Even *Beverly Hills 90210* (considered racy for its time) gave us Donna Martin.[8]

4. I like TV. I've already made five TV references and there are more to come. My brother and I grew up on '80s sitcoms, and to this day we swear there were plenty of life lessons to be learned from this genre of entertainment. For example, everyone always told us not talk to strangers but nothing drove the point home like that episode of *Diff'rent Strokes*[9] when Kimberly and Arnold got kidnapped by the "nice" guy at the grocery store.

5. I make lists. Mindy Kaling from *The Office*[10] (another TV reference—I'll stop counting) used the term "pliest" to describe a piece with a list-y quality.[11] Most of my personal journal entries are in this format and some of that is reflected here in this book.

6. I over-comment. In my footnotes, that is. Do I really think it's necessary to explain that *Single White Female* refers to the '90s thriller film about a roommate who turns into a stalker? Maybe, depending on your audience. I make *a lot* of American pop culture references, some of which may seem obvious, but since I can picture readers ranging broadly across cultures (from my second generation North American cousins and family friends to my relatives in

---

[8] *Beverly Hills 90210* was the young adult drama series of the '90s that focused on teenagers living in the upscale community of Beverly Hills. Donna Martin was a main character who made a decision to abstain from premarital sex.

[9] *Diff'rent Strokes* was an American television sitcom from the late '70s and early '80s about two African-American boys from Harlem who are taken in by a rich, white businessman living on Park Avenue.

[10] *The Office* is an American television comedy series (adapted from the BBC series of the same name) that aired between 2005 and 2013.

[11] Kaling, Mindy, *Is Everyone Hanging Out Without Me?* (New York: Three Rivers Press, 2012).

the Philippines to my Singapore expat circles) as well as generations (from my parents' friends to my peers to my nieces and nephews) I decided to be generous with my footnotes and explanations. Besides, I like providing more context rather than less when telling stories. My friends often tease that "Claire" is short for *Clairification*.

Last disclaimer. I don't know if I'll be able to do all the things I mention in the following pages. And maybe one could argue that I should only write such a book when my kids are grown and I can say I've successfully incorporated these practices. That said, I wanted to do it now for two reasons. First, I have the time (kind of). Maternity leave isn't exactly a sabbatical, but it's the closest thing I've ever had to time off so I'm taking full advantage and doing something I've wanted to do for years. Second, I have the focus. While on leave from work I don't spend my days thinking about how to increase wallet share or grow my customer segment. Spending time with my little ones gives me a chance to be wonderfully wistful and nostalgic. As I watch Isabel fall back asleep in the wee hours of the night I think about what kind of people I hope my children will grow up to be. As I play Thomas the Train with Carlos, I think about my own past, my own childhood and everything I learned from my parents. As I sneak in computer time while both kids are napping, I think about how to capture all these stories and sentiments in writing.

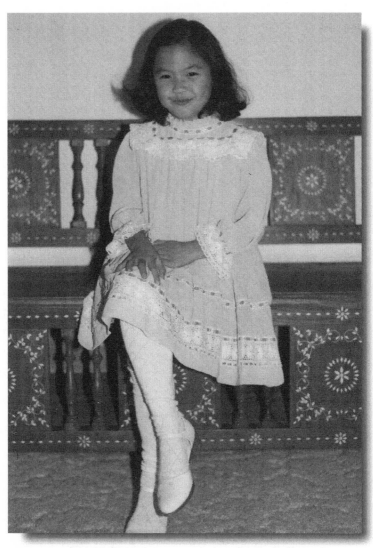

Posing on our *gallinera* (I just learned this piece of Philippine furniture got its name because it's a seat under which chickens were safely kept!) (1983)

New immigrants to Vancouver (1976)

*M*y *parents immigrated* to North America in the 1970s. Like many Filipinos in the US and Canada they were working professionals back home. My mother was an art teacher at International School Manila and my father was pursuing his master's degree at the Asian Institute of Management. They lived a comfortable life in Manila with maids, drivers and even dressmakers. They were newly married and decided to make the move as part of an adventure and because they knew it would probably afford more opportunities for the children they were planning to have.

The first place they landed was Mobile, Alabama. An unlikely destination for new immigrants especially at the time but my mother was presented with a teaching exchange program and it was a good chance to go overseas. My newlywed parents jumped on the opportunity and geared up for their new journey. You would think the biggest adjustments would be the obvious ones like dealing with racial tensions post-Civil Rights movement or being the only Asians in the community but according to my mother these were non-issues. The real change for her was life without help. She didn't know how to cook, she had never before done laundry and she didn't know how to drive. With limited funds, my parents learned to be resourceful very fast. While my mother taught during the day, my father went door to door selling macramé plant hangers that he and my mother had crafted the night before. Overall they had to make do with very little. Of course, it helped that they were from a developing country where recycling was being done well before going green became trendy.

After the teaching assignment ended, my parents drove across country to stay with relatives in California while they applied for immigration status in Canada. They had been advised that US immigration would take far more time plus they had friends in Canada who had recently migrated from the Philippines. After several months and a most compelling immigration interview they were given entry into Vancouver, Canada. Their first plan of action was to secure work. My father often tells the story about how he and my mother looked at the skyline and picked out the tallest building. "They would have jobs." And they were right. It was the Royal Bank of Canada headquarters. My father applied for a role as a management trainee and he got it. One thing about my parents you pick up quickly is that they are smart and practical.

They had me and then my brother, Justin, four years later. These were fun-filled days as my parents and their fellow Filipino immigrants assimilated to life in Canada. Together they formed a tight-knit community and their children all became extended family. Socializing always took place at each other's homes and summer vacations were camping trips maybe an hour drive away. If a relative from the Philippines found a reasonably priced flight to the States it was pretty much assumed that we would pick them up anywhere in continental USA. More than a handful of times my father drove from Vancouver, British Columbia to several parts of California to pick up extended family that would stay with us for months thereafter.

Our house in Coquitlam,[12] British Columbia, became a community center of sorts. Fundraising planning, mahjong nights and *minus one*[13] (pre karaoke) were everyday activities in our kitchen, living and dining rooms. It was the height of the Philippine People Power Revolution[14] and the Marcos regime was under siege. Ninoy Aquino had been assassinated and Filipinos all over the world rallied around the call for democracy. My parents led many of the local political demonstrations and fundraising efforts for the cause so during the months and weeks leading up to the dictator's fall my father was being interviewed by local news stations and TV crews who would show up on our doorstep.

In the late '80s my parents decided to make another big move, this time to New York City. I was devastated to leave the comfort of our tight-knit community where, even at the age of

Our house in Coquitlam, BC (1984)

---

[12] Coquitlam is one of the suburban cities that comprise Metro Vancouver.

[13] Before karaoke machines turned up everywhere, Roberto del Rosario, a prolific Filipino inventor, independently created a music system with accompaniment and a pre-recorded vocals that could be turned up or down on a separate track. The machine became known popularly in the Philippines as *Minus-One* (named after the subtracted vocal channel when turned down).

[14] The People Power Revolution refers to the popular demonstrations in the Philippines between 1983 and 1986. Filipinos take much pride in this nonviolent revolution that led to the departure of President Ferdinand Marcos and the restoration of democracy.

12, I believed my social life had reached an all-time peak. I was a big fish in our tiny elementary Catholic school pond, and I was destined to be popular in high school since I had so many Filipino family friends paving the way. But in their early 40s my parents both felt strongly that they had another adventure to pursue so my mother applied for a job at the United Nations International School (UNIS) and she got it.

In a matter of days after she came back from her job interview, my mother was boarding a plane on a one-way ticket to New York with children in tow as classes were about to begin. You can imagine how shocking it was for all of us especially friends and family (me included) who didn't have the slightest clue that such a change may take place. Even my parents were caught a little unprepared. Before the opportunity came up in New York, they had just opened Sparkles, a small party shop business a few streets away from our home. Months before the move, my mother had enrolled in several courses to pick up skills that would come in handy with her event planning business (many a weekend was spent as a family doing balloon sculpting). When my mother left to start the job at the UNIS, my father stayed behind not just to finish packing but also to live up to the commitments they had accepted including the grand opening of a new factory. He was going to join a real estate firm in New York so his work would have a more flexible start.

On our first year in New York, we lived in a tiny one-bedroom apartment in the heart of Manhattan on 55th Street between Third and Lexington Avenues. We must have adjusted pretty well from a suburban home to a midtown condo because I don't remember any painful transition period (as far as space was concerned; middle school in NYC for me was a whole other story). It did leave us spending plenty of time together—in some ways even more than in Vancouver—because my parents decided to take some time off from Filipino community involvement. Therefore, their social calendar was not as full, and it was often just the four of us.

Eventually I got past my heartbreak over leaving Vancouver and started to embrace New York City. The United Nations International School gave us so many opportunities that to this day I can't believe we got to experience. Student conferences at the UN General Assembly were regular events, our chorus group was invited to perform on TV with teen pop star Debbie Gibson and former UN Secretary General Kofi Annan handed us our graduation diplomas. My parents were astutely aware of this exposure, and it was part of their dream plan for my mother to work at UNIS as a teacher, share the same schedule as her kids and give us the chance to experience truly international New York City living.

I went to Yale for college where doors and networks continued to open. It was there where I met some of the most impressive and inspiring people I know. In many ways these friends helped shape my long-term goals. There was peer pressure to aim high and an expectation to make a meaningful difference to society. In retrospect it may sound young, idealistic and save the world-y but you can't put a value on that kind of influence at such a young age and I'm convinced it is factored into Ivy League tuitions. My parents listened to all my stories and beamed with pride as I pursued exciting opportunities; they just continued to

Yale graduation (1998)

remind me of how fortunate we were and how important it was to give back whenever we could.

After graduation I worked at American Express, where I had interned every summer starting freshman year. I was one of only three undergrads in an 80-person MBA program thanks to a Yale alumnus who convinced HR to give promising college students at shot. One year later I decided to join some of my former classmates who were starting an Internet company and becoming part of what people were calling the "dot com revolution." There were six of us working out of a loft in Williamsburg, Brooklyn, making cold calls, throwing industry parties and raising millions in funding. We were all convinced we'd never have to take a corporate job again. Then the Internet bubble burst and most of us went back to banks, consulting groups and law firms.

I decided to join Citi primarily because I liked the idea of working for such a global company. Since joining the firm, I have taken advantage of every opportunity to work in different businesses and geographies including NYC, Miami, Sao Paulo, Manila, and most recently, Singapore. I started in the US Cards business, which was an easy transition from American Express. I managed to carve a niche for myself by leading the shift from traditional to online marketing and soon I became identified as "high potential." Even more doors opened when I was invited to join a new general management program that would give me a chance to work around the world.

I met my husband, Alex, in Brazil. He joined Citi after completing his MBA at Columbia and he was doing a similar type of management program though focused on finance. In some ways Alex and I couldn't be more different. He was born and raised in a small upstate town with a population of less than a hundred people; my childhood was spent in the Filipino community of Vancouver and then diverse and global New York City. He went to public school all his life and then on to the US Military Academy at West Point; I went to the United Nations International School and then pursued liberal arts at Yale. To a large extent our experiences formed our personalities and anyone who meets us automatically assumes

Attending my ten year reunion at Yale (2008)

we're a case of opposites attract. I have always known, however, that when it comes down to the things that matter most to both of us we couldn't be more similar: How we envision family. How we see ourselves raising kids. How we see ourselves interacting with in-laws. How much time we spend together and how much time we spend apart. How we define balance. How we define success. What we expect from our children. He didn't have the second-generation immigrant experience per se but apparently growing up in a white (well, Irish-Italian-Chilean) blue-collar family in the 1970s and 1980s was not too far off. We are both very grateful for everything we have today, and it's important for us to pass along similar values to our children despite the comfortable upbringing they will likely experience.

My mother on her wedding day (1974)

Family photo (1981)

My parents and their wedding party (1974)

In front of the Twin Towers with my father, my grandmother, Henny and Justin (1990)

Family photo (1983)

Justin and me (1982)

With my mother on my wedding day (2009)

Watching me walk down the aisle with my father (2009)

Finally able to vote (2006)

Speaking at a school conference
at the UN General Assembly (1994)

In front of my cousins' house on Marc Crescent Street.
Front left to right: Me, Natasha, Walid, Faisal, Jay-Jay,
Jon-Jon, Justin. Standing tall at the back is my cousin
Joey and one of his friends (1983)

Outings almost always included three genera-
tions. Back row left to right: Lola Ely, Tita Sally,
Lolo Toni, Lola Adoring, Nana Flor, Amy, Mom,
Tita Hetty; Front row left to right: Henny, me,
Henny's cousin Tammy, Bet, Justin (1983)

My mother and Henny's parents (1983)

Mom in front of Cuba's Hotel Nacional during
one of our family vacations (2003)

On a hike with Alex nearby his home-town in the Adirondacks (2007)

My first visit to Yale (1993)

Family friend and priest Father McGoldrick and his active Filipino parishioners (1983)

Justin and I in a Christmas pageant put on by the University of the Philippines Alumni Association in Vancouver (1984)

Justin and I with childhood friends Leila and Jasmine (1986)

Family photo in Sao Paulo (2006)

MOVIN' ON UP

TAXIS and APPETIZERS

According to my husband and brother, there is a direct correlation between going to Yale and taking taxis. Sure enough, the spouses of my fellow Yale alums seem to agree. "Hey yeah, you're right, Khamen never takes the subway. I guess that's what they teach you at Yale. Your time is too valuable," Khamen's wife, Yara, would tease.

My parents would be similarly amused by my taxi taking frequency. My office was midtown at the Citigroup Center and they lived at Waterside Plaza located just off 23rd Street and FDR Drive. The first time Alex came with me to Waterside we were walking over the footbridge on 25th Street and he said, "Wow, this is unchartered territory." I never thought of it that way since my family had lived there our entire (almost) 20 years in New York. It was conveniently located right next to the UN school so my mother, Justin and I never had to learn the concept of commute. It was the most perfect place to grow up in the city since it was practically a suburb on the island of Manhattan.

A few times a week I would join them after work for dinner at Waterside and they would always ask the rhetorical question, "So how did you get here so fast?" They were well familiar with my rationale that after a long day in the office taking the subway during the height of rush hour, transferring to the bus and then walking a few blocks east would be time-consuming and exhausting. I would much rather pay $10 and jump in a taxi down Second Avenue to get to their place in 10 minutes fresh for great dinner conversation. They seemed to understand my logic; they would just smile and say something like, "Just remember to be thankful that you have the option."

Moments like these seemed to remind my parents of how far we had come. Funny enough, small things like taxis or appetizers were codes for the shift in our lifestyle. "Appetizers" became another inside joke for us. One day when my brother was home from college, we were sitting at a TGIF and flipping through the menu when Justin casually asked, "So what should we do for appetizers?" Our parents chuckled as though it were a punch line. "Wow... appetizers!" my mother said putting on an American accent. Then I caught on. It used to be only on special occasions when you could eat out somewhere and even then you would only order the minimum. Typically you would share a plate with another family member, have a glass of ice water or nurse a small soda, then have coffee and dessert at home. "Appetizers" became a code in our family for being comfortable and living the good life.

Hosting dinner at Waterside (2008)

My parents have always been smart with their spending. Growing up I would just assume we couldn't afford a TV with a remote control or a CD player that many friends were starting to buy. In retrospect, I can see how they could have made those purchases if they had wanted to but instead they chose to save that money for future house down payments or use it on things like violin and piano lessons. Even now they are so practical. They have worked hard, they are reasonably comfortable, and they travel all over the world whether to visit us, to exhibit my mother's artworks, etc. but they still can't bring themselves to buy a new car or a new phone. They are just not necessities as far as my parents are concerned. "All we need is something to get us from Point A to Point B," is one of my father's favorite sayings whenever the topic of a car comes up. To this day, I can't help but notice that our helper's phone is newer and sleeker than anything they've ever owned. My father is still using the iPhone that Alex gave me for Christmas in 2006 and my mother the trusty Nokia flip passed on by one of her nephews. They could have written the books *The Millionaire Next Door*[15] and *Smart Is the New Rich.*[16] Or at least they could have been case studies.

Sometimes my parents assume others are equally discerning when it comes to spending. My brother and I still laugh about the time we met our cousins in the Philippines at one of the local shopping malls. They were running late and after almost an hour past the designated meeting time my father explained, "Before they can get here they first need to take a tricycle to the bus stop and then from the bus they need to take the LRT[17] and then from the LRT they still need to walk or take another tricycle to meet us here."

---

[15] By Thomas J. Stanley and William D. Danko.

[16] By Christine Romans.

[17] Manila Light Rail Transit System, popularly known as the LRT, is the metropolitan rail system serving the Metro Manila area in the Philippines.

As Justin and I pondered this hardship commute, we saw our cousins walking our way. After we greeted them I put on my best empathetic expression and asked, "So how was it getting here?" My cousin Leo responded, "Easy, we just took a taxi."

Not everyone is as smart as my parents when it comes to spending. I take taxis everywhere I go and rationalize that my time is valuable. I justify splurging on a dress as an investment. And I can make the argument that a weekend trip to Stockholm for a wedding is worth it for the experience. But when it comes to my parents' fundamental values and perspective on life, on people, on children, on community, I want to make sure I retain all of these... no matter how many taxis I take.

A summer night at Waterside Plaza (2005)

Justin's birthday was one of the few times I remember dining out—though we didn't order appetizers! (1982)

Group dinner with close friends. From left to right: May, Melissa, Ken, Kristen, me, Danny, Sheldon, Alexis (2005)

View from Waterside Plaza overlooking East River (2005)

DON'T FORGET THE SOAP

S*hortly after I started* working for Citi, I began traveling frequently. This meant early mornings, long flights, time differences and jet lag but it also meant fancy corporate dinners, 5-star hotels, airport lounges and business class. I knew I was starting to get used to all the perks when I stopped taking the extra soap and shampoo bottles from my hotel room. It had become second nature for me to do a morning sweep of the bathroom toiletries before leaving each day to ensure my supply was replenished when the room was made. By the time check out day came, I was about ready to start my own mini mart. When I got home I'd put them aside in a shopping bag and before I knew it they'd be packed away in a *balikbayan* box that our family would send back to the Philippines.

During my assignment in Brazil I lived in the Marriott Executive Apartments so I hit the jackpot in soap and shampoo bottles. After the first few weeks, however, I couldn't be bothered to save the soap and shampoo anymore. Then my family came to visit for Christmas. I was happy and excited to show them Sao

Paulo, where I lived, where I worked and what I did. We had a blast and they were thrilled to see what my life was like in this new city. But I'll always remember my mother's tone of disbelief when she realized I hadn't been putting aside the soap and shampoo for us to send to the Philippines ("Not even just once a week?").

At first I thought it was a lot of fuss over a little soap but very soon I came to realize it wasn't just about the toiletries. It was about thinking of others. Mini bottles of shampoos and body wash may have become customary for me but my mother reminded me that they were still a treat for others. When she gave the "fancy" soap to people back home she would wrap them beautifully in

Dad and Justin at the Marriott Executive Apartments in Sao Paulo (2006)

tissue and ribbon usually alongside another *pasalubong*[18] and they would feel special and remembered.

I ended up incorporating a once-a-week-putting-away-the-soap routine into my new year's resolutions. From then on, it became a running joke in our family. My mother would end each conversation with, "Don't forget the soap!" It turned into a standard family reminder right up there with, "Get enough rest" and "Remember to pray." Putting away the soap once a week served as a good reminder not to take anything for granted no matter how big or small. No matter how busy or caught up I would get.

Enjoying the luxurious hotel bathroom accommodations (2005)

---

[18] *Pasalubong* is the Filipino tradition of a homecoming gift. *Pasalubong* can be any gift or souvenir brought for family, loved ones or friends after being away for a period of time.

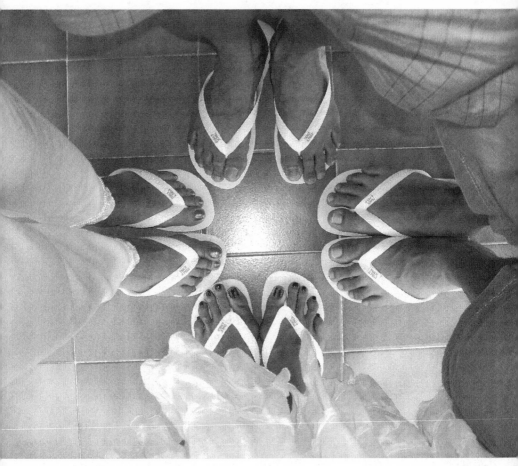

Brazilian Havaianas (2005)

GIVING BACK

NOT THE TYPICAL BIRTHDAY PRESENT

At one point when my mother was praying for a healthy baby, she made a deal with God. "If I'm blessed with a healthy baby I promise I'll do everything I can to help those who are not." Around this time her aunt, Tita Elma,[19] had become involved in a major undertaking to establish a school for disabled children in her local province. It was a project close to her heart as her daughter Eileen had Down syndrome. Tita Elma lived in San Pablo, Laguna, a country town about an hour and a half outside Manila, and there were no school options for children like Eileen anywhere in the vicinity so she decided to do something about it.

Ever since I can remember, for every occasion that my brother and I celebrated, my mother would send a contribution in our names to the School of Love and Hope. It's Justin's birthday and we're having a party—let's make sure the School of Love and Hope kids get some cake and ice cream too. It's Valentine's

---

[19] *Tita* means "Aunt" and *Tito* means "Uncle."

Day and we're making Valentine's Day cards—let's make sure the School of Love and Hope kids have art supplies as well.

I remember it dawning on me one day that Justin and I never got birthday presents from our parents. There was always a cake and almost always a party but no big box to open from my mom and dad. I realized it one day after my friend Marina asked, "What did your parents get you? The Barbie Dream House? My Little Pony Castle?" That's when I asked my mother, "Why don't Justin and I get presents from you when it's our birthday?" My mother answered, "We gave you a party."

"That's my present? I mean like a toy."

"You get a lot of toy presents from everyone else. Our gift to you is a donation in your name to the School of Love and Hope. Because of you those children who have very little will also have a celebration today. One day you'll realize what a special gift that is."

Of course, we had minimal appreciation for what that meant at the time but as we got older and especially once we visited the school we became fully aware of what a unique privilege it is to be part of such a special mission our entire lives. I was watching an interview with Oprah recently and realized she felt a similar gratitude from children after she opened *Oprah Winfrey Leadership for Girls* in South Africa. My parents have been giving us this gift since our first birthday. Even when we visit today some of the kids tell us, "We have been celebrating your birthday since 1976."

When Tita Elma opened the school doors in 1974 there were 37 children and 5 teachers. Today the school has over 200 children who attend from all across the province and they are the only complete special education school in the region catering to all kinds of handicaps from preparatory level to high school. The school's rondalla[20] comprised of 32 hearing-impaired children

---

[20] The rondalla is an ensemble of stringed instruments played with the plectrum or pick and generally known as plectrum instruments. The word *rondalla* is from the Spanish ronda, meaning "serenade."

School of Love and Hope Rondalla (2013)

have competed (and won) in regional contests, the students have participated in almost all Special Olympics (domestic as well as international), and the school was recently accredited by the Philippine government and now receives funding.[21]

Tita Elma's school has continued to remain top of mind for me and Justin. Throughout high school and college we organized fundraisers for School of Love and Hope through student clubs and Filipino organizations.[22] My parents and I actually watched Justin come into his own while organizing a Filipino Cultural Evening at UNIS to benefit School of Love and Hope. I remember this coming-of-age transformation vividly. Even though he constantly had a big smile on his face, Justin had always been on the shy side. As his big sister I would often speak on his behalf on matters big and small whether changing an order at a restaurant, negotiating a comic book trade with our cousin Arvi or asking my parents'

---

[21] More information about this amazing school can be found on their website at http://www.schoolofloveandhopesped.com/.

[22] My efforts would be through *Kasama*, the Filipino Club of Yale, and Justin's would be through *MUFASA*, the McGill University Filipino and Asian Student Association.

Visiting School of Love and Hope (Pagibig at Pagasa in Tagalog) (2013)

permission to do something. However, after a visit to School of Love and Hope one summer, Justin became inspired to take initiative and make a direct personal contribution to the cause.

One evening over family dinner he raised his idea of hosting a Filipino Cultural Evening at UNIS whereby all proceeds could go to the school. We had grown up watching my parents put on these events in Vancouver so we all knew what kind of production would be involved (cultural dances, music, Filipino food spread, etc.) and my parents and I were ready to make it a family affair. Organizing the Filipino Cultural Evening pushed Justin way outside his comfort zone. He was taking center stage (literally and figuratively) inviting prominent members of the United Nations community, coordinating with music and dance groups and, of course, preparing his opening speech to kick off the event. The event was a smashing success, and Justin exceeded not

Tita Elma giving us a tour of the school (2013)

only his fundraising goals but also all expectations around how much of an impact he could make in one evening.

Once in college Justin continued his efforts to raise money for the school. In fact, MUFASA, the McGill University Filipino and Asian Student Association, still continues to send money to School of Love and Hope years after Justin graduated. And today when I tell my mother about what we have planned for Carlos' birthday party she'll say, "Great. And then you can match what you spend in a contribution to School of Love and Hope."

Kasama: The Filipino Club of Yale (1996)

Performing "Pandanggo Sa Ilaw" a traditional Filipino dance during Barrio Fiesta hosted by Kasama (1997)

Outside Malacañang Palace after meeting President Corazon Aquino (1986)

TOY FOR JOY

My parents were constantly coming up with ways to give back whether it was to the Filipino community around them or to the artist circles back in the Philippines. Not only with money but with time, with innovative ideas, and with whatever knowledge, skills or networks they had. After the People Power Revolution, our family had the opportunity to meet President Corazon Aquino on one of our trips back to the Philippines. It was a private audience meeting,[23] and we all sat around what felt like her living room even though it was Malacañang Palace.[24] My brother and I had been hearing about "Cory" and her late husband for literally our entire lives so even at 12 and eight years of age we had a relatively good appreciation for the significance of this meeting.

---

[23] A formal meeting that takes place between a head of state and another person at the invitation of the head of state.

[24] The Malacañang Palace is the official residence and principal workplace of the President of the Philippines.

Family photo with President Corazon Aquino (1986)

President Aquino thanked my parents for all their support from overseas. Filipinos around the world putting pressure on local embassies and consulates had been critical in sending across a message to the Marcos administration as well as to influential political allies such as the United States. When my parents asked the president what else they could do to help her from Canada she told them about one particular project in which she could use their support. While she was primarily focused on alleviating poverty, she had one idea specifically related to children. There were people working on providing food and clothing for the poor—no question those were absolute necessities. At the same time, she explained, if she could get her wish the poor children would also be able to experience the pure delight of a toy that Christmas. It sounded so simple but bear in mind that at that time, before the mass production of goods in China, even relatively comfortable

families would give their children
only one toy during the holiday.

My parents went back to
Vancouver and started a fundraising
drive called "Toy for Joy." They had
already established the Philippine
HELP Foundation[25] so this effort
became one of their projects.
Children of their friends got
involved as well and we did
everything from organizing car
washes to selling raffle tickets
in shopping malls to hosting
high school dances. We even
came up with a name for the
HELP Foundation kids: JAM
4 HELP. JAM was short for
"Junior Adult Members," and

we were very pleased with ourselves for being
able to incorporate the cool numerical "4" into our name. JAM
was one of the reasons I was so woeful about leaving Vancouver
when we did. Founding members were all part of the who's who of
Vancouver's high school social scene. My best friend Henny and
I were not even 12, but we were involved in the planning of what
felt like the party of the century, Summer Jam '88 (Henny came up
with that one). For kids trying their first attempt at fundraising, we
raised a significant sum of money. Sure, JAM was a built-in way to
socialize (many of us had relatively strict parents so hanging out in
shopping malls was generally not allowed and more than a handful
of us weren't permitted to go to dances), but more importantly
we learned at an early age how much could be accomplished
when people—even young people—organized themselves for a
common purpose.

---

[25] Shortly after the People Power Revolution, my parents and friends founded the
Philippine HELP Foundation (Human Endeavor to Lessen Poverty) to continue the great
fundraising work they had started.

HELP Foundation camping trip (1988)

Today my mother is an established artist, and her schedule is booked with exhibits and openings around the world. It amazes me how much time she is still able to dedicate to other artists whether giving exposure to up-and-coming painters and printmakers from the Philippines, leading the Society of Philippine American Artists[26] or facilitating workshops in different locations for those with limited resources. She often says that while she doesn't have the financial means to help everyone she wants to, she can use her network, her organizational skills and whatever talent she has to give back whenever she can.

Philippine HELP Foundation fundraising event (1988)

---

[26] SPAA was founded in 1995 as an organization to promote Philippine American visual artists. It has grown to become one of the biggest advocates for Filipino artists living in North America.

PEOPLE SKILLS

*W*hen my mother had her first solo art show, it was a big deal for all of us. We knew she was a talented artist even though her full-time job was teaching during our early childhood. Being a teacher at the United Nations International School allowed her to have the same schedule as her kids, paid the bills and demonstrated she was naturally great with children. That said, we were cognizant that her true passion was her art though she put it on hold in order to focus on family. While she didn't pursue her own art career as we were growing up, she found ways to continuously incorporate art into her life whether it was through organizing exhibits for students or helping emerging Filipino artists present their pieces in Canada and the US.

There was one particular incident (or rather, accident) that pushed my mother to pursue her art career shortly after we moved to New York. On her way to school one day she had a bad fall and bumped her head on uneven pavement. She was sent immediately to NYU Hospital where she was examined by a neurologist named Dr. Neophytides. He confirmed everything would be OK but strongly advised my mother to spend a few weeks at home to recover. As the conversation shifted to what she did and where she worked, Dr. Neophytides mentioned he would be sending his daughter, Alexis, to UNIS the following school year. Soon after they realized their daughters were the same age and my mother promised that we would look out for Alexis when September came. As it turned out, Alexis and I were in the same homeroom class and we became instant friends.

During my mother's disability leave, one of her artist friends happened to be staying with us while in New York for a group show. Myrna Reyes and my mother were fellow students at the University of the Philippines School of Fine Arts. As Tita Myrna worked on her pieces during the day, my mother began picking up the paintbrush again too. She quickly realized how much she missed doing her art and decided to enroll in a few courses at the School of Visual Arts (SVA). My mother returned to work a few weeks later but continued to pursue her art in the evenings. She would spend eight hours a day with 15 five-year-olds, come home to have dinner with the family, and then she was off to the SVA studio for a couple more hours to work on

My mother at the UN with Ambassador Hilario Davide and Ambassador and Mrs. Libran Cabactulan (2008)

her pieces. She had taken a particular interest in printmaking and explored all types of techniques using this medium.

In the early '90s she had her first solo exhibits scheduled at the Philippine Center in New York City and the Ayala Museum in Manila. By this time she had started to make some influential connections in the art world including Agnes Gund, the President Emerita of the Museum of Modern Art, who would later write the preface to my mother's book.[27] Many of the people who were helping her organize the art show suggested she ask one of the big names to open the exhibits. My mother had someone else in mind. Sister Araceli had been one of the teachers at the College of the Holy Spirit, where my mother attended elementary and high school. She had seen potential in my mother as a child and offered to give her free art lessons on Saturday mornings. My mother still considers this time with Sister Araceli an important influence in her decision to take up Fine Arts in college. She also believed that being asked to open the exhibit would mean the world to Sister Araceli but be just another request to others.

At the Philippine Center with Agnes Gund, President Emerita of the Museum of Modern Art (1998)

My mother has this general approach to people. She observes that those in current positions of power often have so much attention and countless invitations that one more usually makes no difference. She tends to give her focus to people when they need it most, for example, when a new widow is adjusting to life without her husband or a newly retired government official is

[27] *Profound Afterglow:* The Prints of Lenore RS Lim

With Nana Flor (1983)

adjusting to life without his title. She used to tell me about one of her relatives who was a prominent politician in the Philippines. For years she watched crowds vying for his attention at every function and colleagues sending gifts to his family on each holiday. All of this attention stopped once he no longer held his status. It was then that my mother would go out of her way to visit his home, invite him to functions and greet him for the holidays. He lost his prestigious position with the government but gained VIP status with my mother.

She has this way of honing in where it matters most and being there when it counts. When Justin was born, my parents sponsored someone from the Philippines to come to Canada as our helper. Nana Flor came from a small province outside Manila and was referred to us through a family friend. She was single and without children, but her sole purpose of going to Canada was to help support her family, in particular her nieces and nephews. I remember Nana Flor as a strong-willed sometimes scary figure (who was far less strict with boys[28]) but my parents describe her as very quiet if not timid when she first arrived. She was with us just a few months before her 30th birthday when my mother decided to throw her a party. She invited all of our family friends, arranged for a cake and prepared a special menu. A couple of days before the party, however, my parents were invited to a big celebration for one of the high ranking officers at the Philippine Consulate that was scheduled for the same night as Nana Flor's birthday. He was just an acquaintance of my parents at the time but some of their friends thought they should make a point to go since he would be a good contact in the future. A few of my mother's friends tried to convince her that a party for our helper wasn't necessary. My mother told them that they should feel free to attend the event at the Philippine Consulate but she would still go ahead with Nana Flor's party. "He won't even know we're there but Nana Flor will always remember this birthday." She was right. My mother went

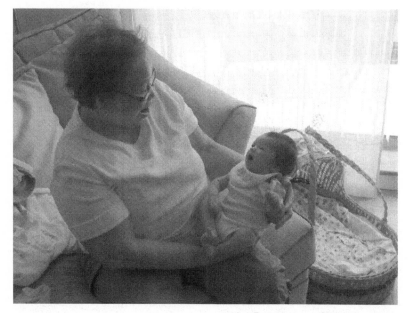

Nana Flor with my son, Carlos, 30 years later.

---

[28] Justin and my cousins Faisal and Walid were allowed to stay up late with her and watch grown up television dramas *Miami Vice* and *Moonlighting* while Natasha and I were sent up to bed at 8:00 p.m. sharp and couldn't make a sound (Nana Flor would remind us that she would be listening to the child monitor).

forward with her original plans, and all of our friends decided to join us as well. Nana Flor was so touched that everyone would go through the trouble for her. She told us that she had never had a birthday party before and it was a day she would never forget.

Nana Flor continued to remain a big part of our lives and her welfare a considerable focus of my mother's attention. Like most Filipino domestic helpers, she had family in the Philippines depending on her income. While my mother helped her figure out ways to send money back home, she took time to educate Nana Flor about saving money for herself as well. She also helped her earn extra income through part-time babysitting, which she would do on weekday afternoons.

My mother recalls that one day as she was picking me up from kindergarten she noticed another Filipina mother who seemed stressed and hurried as she was doing the same. They got to talking and my mother learned the woman was a doctor who had her own practice. Every day she had to jump out of work to pick up her two daughters, drop them off with a babysitter and then go back to see patients. It turned out that her younger daughter, Leila, was in my class and the two of us were friends. Her older daughter, Jasmine, was in the second grade and the three of us got along nicely. My mother had a thought: she could pick up Leila and Jasmine when she came for me and Nana Flor could look after all of us for a few hours until Dr. Albrecht (Tita Ruth) was done with her day. Nana Flor would make extra money, and Dr. Albrecht wouldn't have to run out in the middle of the day. She ran the suggestion by Nana Flor who was more than eager about the plan. We were easy self-sufficient kids who stayed out of trouble. Between 3:00 and 6:00 p.m. we would do homework and then ride our bikes, run through sprinklers or make up another game outside. Dr. Albrecht was ecstatic and so grateful to my mother. When Justin and I learned that Leila and Jasmine would be coming home with us every day we were overjoyed to have playmates every afternoon. It was an ideal setup for everyone. On many days Henny and her sisters would come over from down the street and it was one big after school program.

In addition to facilitating extra income for her, my parents also opened up a retirement savings plan for Nana Flor and made sure she was registered for all the benefits for which she qualified with the Canadian government. Eventually she was able to buy a one-bedroom apartment in Vancouver as she was eligible for subsidized housing. Eventually Nana Flor sold her condo, made a big profit and used the money to build a house in her province for her siblings. Before we moved to New York, my mother had set up Nana Flor with a job at a retail food outlet owned by a family friend. My parents continued to stay in close touch with her after we moved away. By this point she had become like extended family not just to us but to all our closest friends. My mother would make sure she was invited to someone's Christmas dinner or Easter lunch and to this day I get a reminder from my mother to call Nana Flor every year on her birthday.

My son, Carlos, was born 30 years after we first welcomed Nana Flor into our home. The relationship between her and my

Some of my mother's closest friends and biggest supporters during her recent art exhibit at Tally Beck Contemporary in New York City: Dad, Fiel Zabat, Dan Santamaria, Devraj Dakoji (2013)

mother was equally strong in spite of the fact that it had been 22 years since she worked for our family. When my maternity leave ended and Nana Flor heard I was returning to work just three months after the baby was born (standard in the US but she was used to Canada where maternity leave is one year) she offered to come to New York and help look after Carlos. Of course, I loved the idea (who wouldn't?) but I didn't want her to go through that much trouble as it would involve unnecessary travel and time away from her home. She insisted on coming, and I knew she saw it as an opportunity to do something nice for my mother and our family.

Today my parents spend their time between New York, Vancouver, Manila and most recently Singapore. If you ask my mother what she has planned the first few days of a trip, you would never know she was about to exhibit 100 pieces of work at a national gallery or lead the centennial anniversary celebration of her alma mater. She receives dozens of invitations weeks in advance of her arrival but before doing anything else she has lined up visits with all the elderly friends of her late mother. She never forgets that Tita Anita always went out of her way to pick up my Lola while she stayed with us in Vancouver. Or that Tita Sally and Tita Lily provided great companionship after Lola became a widow. "They need the company the most. For so-and-so I'll be just one of many appointments today. For others I'm the only engagement in their schedules for weeks. And they will get many stories out of my visit that they can tell others. I'll tell them news about you and Justin that they'll be first to know. They'll feel special being able to share it with their families. Just imagine, for so many years they were the matriarch of the family—their role was so important—and then one day it's like no one needs them anymore." She refers to these gestures as "corporal works of mercy."[29] We just refer to them as "so Mom."

---

[29] There are seven corporal works of mercy in the Catholic faith: feed the hungry, give drink to the thirsty, shelter the homeless, clothe the naked, visit the sick, visit the imprisoned, and bury the dead. My mother references these regularly.

(Right page) Lenore RS Lim: *Baro at Saya*, Lithography, chine colle, 44" x 30", 2010

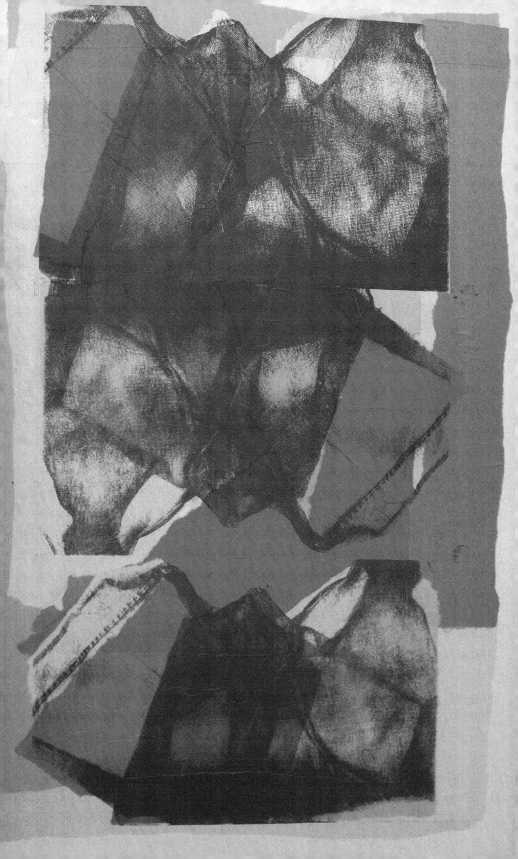

Taking Nana Flor out to the ballgame when she came to stay with us in New York City (2011)

Sister Araceli as guest of honor during my mother's art exhibit at Ayala Museum in the Philippines (1991)

Secretary General Kofi Annan admiring my mother's art at the UN World Women Conference (2000)

My mother with President Benigno "Noynoy" Aquino III taken at an art exhibit at Manila Hotel to commemorate the 4th death anniversary of President Corazon Aquino (2013)

With close relatives attending my mother's art show at the
Cultural Center of the Philippines (2011)

My mother's art show in Abu Dhabi. Standing here with Abdulla Al Amir, Director of
Culture and Arts Institute, Ambassador and Mrs. Libran Cabactulan (2008)

Photo taken while my family was visiting me in Brazil (2005)

TOP **100** FRIENDS

My brother and I always get a little kick out of my mother saying things like, "Of course, you know Ching. She's one of my best friends." We find it so remarkable because she really does consider this person to be one of her closest friends; it just so happens she has about a hundred of them. And they're not merely acquaintances. She has lifelong friends from every stage of her life. Best friends from College of the Holy Spirit where she studied from elementary to high school, best friends from University of the Philippines School of Fine Arts, best friends from International School Manila where she taught after graduating college, best friends from Vancouver and best friends from New York (different circles that include the UNIS community, the Christian Life Community, the Philippine Consulate, the Society of Philippine American Artists, etc.). And then there are all the friends she picks up in passing along the way. It's not uncommon for us to be out somewhere new and look over to find my mother in deep conversation with a total stranger.

Just the other day we were at a kiddie gym in Singapore doing a class with Carlos. "Is your mom crying over there with one of the instructors?" Alex asked as he helped Carlos with a somersault. I turned around to see my mother patting dry tears and handing a tissue to the young woman who signed us in. It turned out the instructor is the niece of Sister Araceli (the teacher who had given my mother free art lessons when she was in elementary school) and they were sharing fond memories of the nun who passed away a few years back. Who knows how they made the tie but I've stopped asking because these occurrences happen all too often. I don't comprehend how exactly my mother does it but she naturally draws people in and once she makes a connection she stays in touch with everyone who has touched her life in a big or small way.

My first baby, Carlos, was born on a hot summer day in August at Lenox Hill Hospital on the Upper East Side of Manhattan. He was more than a week overdue so I was going into the hospital to be induced. Alex and I arrived midnight on a Saturday and if all went according to plan we would have our baby sometime Sunday afternoon (just making the cutoff date for a Leo, which we secretly wanted).[30] But alas, all didn't go according to plan—the Pitocin didn't bring on contractions and I never started dilating. By late afternoon my doctor gave us a choice. She could go ahead and do a C-section since I was already deep in hospital procedures or they could disconnect me from everything, release me and then I could come back the day after tomorrow and they would try to induce me again. It was our first baby and we were hoping for a normal delivery so I spent the next three hours signing release papers and being examined before I was finally discharged. We joined our parents and Justin who were waiting in the hospital lobby and went out for Thai food around the corner.

---

[30] Alex and I have come to the conclusion that some of the strongest people we know are Leos. Plus, Leos have won three of the last five US presidential races (this includes Bill Clinton and Barack Obama).

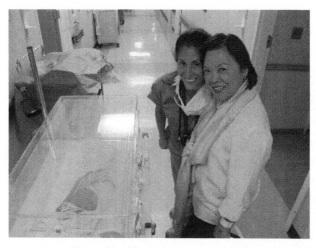

Mom and Very Nice Nurse (and the baby blue pashmina!) (2013)

We came back to the hospital midnight that Tuesday (our hopes for a Leo baby all but forgotten) and started the whole inducing process again. This time I felt it working and my water finally broke in the middle of the night. I remember one of the nurses exclaiming, "Hooray! This baby's going to come out, after all!" I was in pain due to the contractions but I was so excited to be making progress on the delivery that it didn't seem to matter. By the time morning came I had dilated to 8 centimeters—only 2 to go until I would start pushing. My doctor was doing the rounds and told me to prepare for the "hard part." But when she came by again an hour later there had been no more progress. I was still at 8 centimeters. Shortly after the nurses noticed my temperature rising. "Oh no," I heard one of them say. She saw my concerned look and said, "Don't worry. We'll check again in a few minutes and hopefully it will pass." When the fever didn't pass she explained to me the procedures they would have to follow. Once the baby was born they would have to send him or her (we didn't know the sex) directly to the NICU (intensive care unit) to make sure everything was all right. Except for my slight temperature everything seemed fine with me so it shouldn't be a problem but they had to follow standard procedures.

I never ended up getting to 10 centimeters and so we needed to prepare for a C-section. As the nurses were removing the catheter and everything else connected to me they realized that the baby had been positioned on my bladder, and the pressure had stopped me from urinating and resulted in my fever. Mystery solved. But the baby would still need to go directly to the NICU.

Things weren't about to start going smoothly. We tried to plow through the red tape and get Carlos transferred to the well nursery but no luck. We kept a good attitude though, thankful for our healthy baby but wishing we could see him more than a few minutes every three hours. It was clear that he was healthy and did not belong in the NICU, but we realized there were hospital procedures to be followed even if we couldn't understand them. To make matters worse, however, there was one particular nurse in the NICU who was being extremely hostile. "C'mon, we don't have all day. Give me the baby," she would say as I was trying to nurse him for the very first time. She would give me all of two minutes before saying she needed to give the baby a bottle, i.e., formula before kicking me out of the room. When Alex had to leave the following day to attend his brother's wedding upstate (you can't time these things) the nurse antagonistically commented, "I guess he doesn't think he needs to be here."

I held it together until the day I was scheduled to be released. When Antagonistic Nurse said, "There's no way I'm going to approve this baby going home with you today," I lost it. After almost a week in the hospital, two rounds of inducing labor, an emergency C-section, a fever that sent my healthy baby to the intensive care unit and four days at the mercy of Antagonistic Nurse, I couldn't believe there was even a chance that I would not be able to take my baby home. The only thing getting me through the last four days was the thought that my baby and I would be going home and we wouldn't have to think about the NICU or Antagonistic Nurse ever again.

My mother was there each step of the way and watched as I tried to talk to whoever would listen to ensure my baby could leave with me that day. I was having no luck at all but thanks to one very nice pashmina and one very nice nurse things turned around. Earlier in the week, somewhere between 2 and 8 centimeters, my mother was waiting for the elevator when a very nice nurse complimented her on the baby blue pashmina she was wearing. That started a conversation and it didn't take them long to make a connection about a mutual friend (a former Filipina nurse who had worked at the same hospital). Later that day, somewhere between the operating room and the NICU, my mother saw our baby being rolled through the hallway and Very Nice Nurse happened to be walking by. "That's my grandson!" my mother said proudly. Very Nice Nurse oohed and aahed the way you're supposed to when someone points out their baby and even took a picture with my mother.

It turns out Very Nice Nurse was one of the senior nurses in the hospital. We learned so when my mother bumped into her once more the day I was being discharged. They struck up a conversation and my mother mentioned the difficulty I was having trying to ensure my baby could leave the hospital with me. She was curious and asked to see the baby. She came by the NICU as I was holding Carlos. She looked at him, the file, and then at the baby again and said, "There's no reason he shouldn't be transferred to the well nursery. Once he's there they'll discharge him today." I was so happy to hear those words I wanted to cry. I didn't know what influence Very Nice Nurse had but she was speaking with such authority it was comforting. She took Antagonistic Nurse to the side, and they talked. She then came back saying that she would talk to the doctor who runs the NICU and assured us that we wouldn't have to worry. Just like that and we were on our way home with Baby Carlos, and all was right with the world.

Weeks later, once we were settled back home my mother came by one day with a new baby blue pashmina still wrapped in plastic. She said it would be good for me to send it to Very Nice Nurse who was so helpful when we were trying to leave the hospital. It wasn't even a second thought for my mother, but it struck me as such a great idea. Sure, I had reflected on how nice she had been and how grateful I was to have had her help

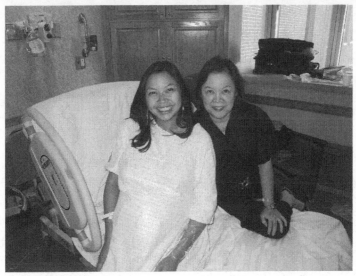

Waiting for her first grandchild (2010)

that desperate day. Maybe it had crossed my mind to send her a thank you note, but chances are that I wouldn't get around to it. My mother always follows through on these ideas and the gestures never go unnoticed, which is part of why she has so many friends.

Her personal network is not about making contact with the most important people in the room. She develops real relationships with people who positively impact her life and vice versa. Sometimes it can be the President of the Museum of

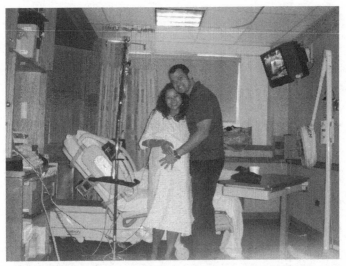

Here for the long haul (2010)

Modern Art and sometimes it can be the nun who gave her free art lessons. She reaches out because of genuine interest in people and not just when she needs something. These kinds of relationships are lifelong and they have proven to be invaluable in good times and bad. As a result, so many people jump at the opportunity to help in any project she may have whether it's publishing a book for emerging Filipino artists, planning her daughter's wedding or putting up her own art exhibit.

Recently one of our family friends asked my mother for help in promoting his wife's novel. He had seen on many occasions how my mother had obtained coverage not only for her own art shows but also for those of other Filipino artists. She had PR friends helping with press releases, contacts at the Philippine Consulate assisting with launch events, graphic designers doing invitations and curators setting up the exhibits, all of these pro bono. Her friend was hoping to leverage the same people for help. I could see it was difficult for my mother to provide a playbook on how to promote something not because she didn't want to share her contacts but because she knew many of these contacts might not be as willing to help. Her relationships with these people have been built over decades and couldn't be replicated overnight.

My mother planned my father's 50th birthday party. Close friend and concert pianist Raul Sunico graciously hosted at his New York home. Top left to right: Tito Raul, Tito Benny, Tita Bella, Tita Angie, Tita Cora, Tito Mars. Bottom left to right: Tita Nanette, Tita Baby, Tito Louis, Tita Lea, Father Dan, Dad, Mom, Tito Centee, Tita Tessie and Justin in the middle—I was away at college (1997)

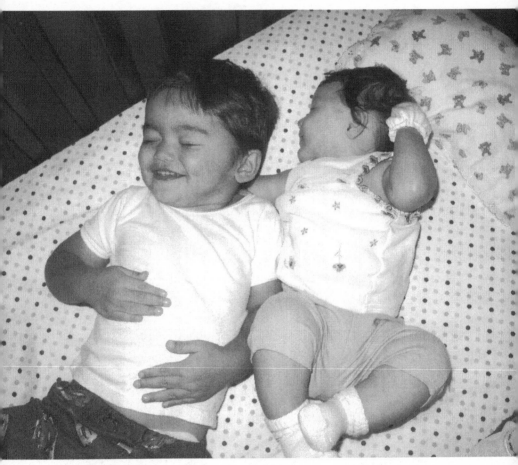

Little loves (2013)

NO REGRETS
(WELL, ALMOST NO REGRETS)

For someone so positive my mother can sound surprisingly morbid at times. Alex, Justin and I constantly exchange looks of disbelief after she says something like, "I used to think when it's my time, it's my time but now that I have grandchildren I hope to make it longer. I want to see Carlos go to kindergarten..." Carlos is two and a half so kindergarten is practically next year. "Low bar! Low bar!" Alex will exclaim, "Let's aim to see Carlos go to college!" Without fail, whenever we're watching a movie or hearing about someone sick whose family is doing everything they can to keep that person alive, my mother will say, "If it happens to me, just let me die." We teasingly call her, "Lenore 'Pull-the-Plug' RS Lim."

She has always seemed almost too at peace with the idea of dying. When giving birth to Justin in 1980 she experienced a serious complication immediately following her cesarean. She began losing blood fast and even the (seven pint) blood transfusion didn't seem to be enough. When my father asked the doctors how serious her condition was they told him she had a 50/50 chance of surviving. My parents said their just-in-case goodbyes before my mother went into the operating room for the second time. They prayed together, my mother asked my father to take care of the children and then she thought to herself, "Well, if I don't make it I'll be in heaven and I'll see them from above. At least I won't worry anymore about falling behind on my thank you cards and other correspondence." I kid you not!

Over a decade later the complications from her delivery resurfaced this time in the form of Hepatitis C. Unfortunately the blood transfusion from years ago had transferred more than just blood. In the early '80s they were not testing for HIV or Hepatitis C, and as it turned out my mother had contracted the latter. Apparently the virus was already very active when it was found so the doctors had no choice but to discuss serious options. I remember still being in shock while trying to understand the waitlist procedure for a liver transplant. I couldn't believe what was happening. My mother took it all in and barely seemed fazed. She continued to pray as she normally did and said things like, "When it's your time, it's your time."

I'm sure part of her peace on the subject of death is her good old Catholic faith (everything happens for a reason), but I'm also convinced there's more to it than that. She lives her life in such a way that if she dies tomorrow there is nothing she would regret not having done today. For some people, living life with no regrets means taking that chance to skydive while they're young and without kids. For my mother, it means not missing an opportunity to make those she cares about happy. It's why she doesn't forget to send a follow-up thank you to anyone who positively impacts her life, why she never puts off a visit to someone she thinks could use one and why she reflects on each day to make sure she's done something meaningful, which could be something as simple as calling a friend who's fallen ill.

I once asked my mother if she has any regrets. She thought about it for a moment and answered, "When Robert Jongco stayed with us…" It still amuses me when I think of this remorse hanging over her head. Robert is the youngest child of my parents' friends Benny and Nanette Jongco. His older sister Kristen and I had become very close during our time at Yale and as a result our families had become even closer. The Jongcos lived in South Orange, New Jersey so when Robert got into Xavier High School in New York City his parents were making arrangements for him to stay in the city during the week. They had recently purchased a midtown apartment as an investment and the plan was for Robert to live there with their oldest child, Melissa, who was studying medicine at New York Medical College. The apartment wasn't ready when Robert's school term was about to begin so my parents offered to have him stay with them in the meantime.

At this point my mother was undergoing Interferon treatment[31] for Hepatitis C. In layman's terms, Interferon is a lot like chemotherapy for cancer patients (basically in that it sucks). I knew how badly she was feeling and under no other circumstance would she want anyone staying with them during this time. An exception was made because of my mother's closeness to the Jongcos. Robert moved into the room of Justin (who was then away at McGill University in Montreal) and boarded with my parents until Thanksgiving. I happened to be living there during this time in between dorm room and first apartment post-college. As far as I could tell Robert was perfectly happy and at home. He would wake up around 6:30 in the morning, get dressed in his school uniform, make his lunch sandwich and have his morning cereal, and then take the bus to school right outside our lobby. In the afternoon he would come back, fix himself a snack, do his homework and then join us for dinner. When Robert talks about his time with my parents today, he recounts fond memories (my dad's chicken curry, my mom's arts and crafts time—there were a couple of nights when we sat around the table making handmade Christmas cards) but if you hear my mother talk about this period it sounds as though Robert had been living alone in a dark and dreary apartment. She regrets not being able to add colorful garnishes to his meals, not being able to get up early every day

---

[31] Most common medical treatment for viral hepatitis.

and set the table a la bed and breakfast style. Not being able to add to his brown lunch bag a fruit cut up in decorative shapes. She knows the full experience she could have given Robert while he stayed with us, and it troubles her to this day that she was sick at the time and incapable.

Recently a number of our elder family friends passed away, most of them in their late 80s and 90s at this time. I often see my aunts and uncles lamenting that they did not visit so-and-so enough, feeling guilty they never got a chance to greet them on their last birthday and scurrying around to make arrangements back to the Philippines to at least attend the services. My mother mourns their loss but there is calmness in her grieving since she has no regrets about anything she might have done. Just by watching her I am constantly reminded of how important it is to do what you can for people when you have the opportunity since it won't always be there.

All the "kids" at a recent gathering at the Jongcos' place (2012)

With the Jongcos at Jin Fong Chinatown (2012)

In front of our favorite Chinatown Ice Cream Factory (2012)

BALANCE

UN–TIGER[32] MOM

My *mother* *was* *different* *from* *most* *immigrant* *parents* when it came to school. She didn't push us too hard. In fact, she barely nudged us. She claims it's because she could see we were already putting pressure on ourselves to achieve but there's something oddly amusing about your mother shutting off the lights and deciding you've studied enough.

"You're already doing everything you can so whatever the outcome is fine. You don't have to be at the top. It's more important to be balanced." My mother would go on to explain how she would much prefer her children to be well-rounded kids who were respectful to their parents and kind to others than straight A students on a one-dimensional track. We would laugh out loud and she would tell us not to underestimate the importance of this balance.

There wasn't a term for it back then but let's just say she was very pleased years later when Daniel Goleman first published his book *Emotional Intelligence: Why It Can Matter More Than IQ* to

---

[32] Reference to Amy Chua's book, *Battle Hymn of the Tiger Mother*

Cross Campus Library at Yale (1997)

argue why qualities such as self-awareness, motivation, empathy and social skills could be even more important than IQ. "If your emotional abilities aren't in hand, if you don't have self-awareness, if you are not able to manage your distressing emotions, if you can't have empathy and have effective relationships, then no matter how smart you are, you are not going to get very far," she once quoted directly from the book.[33]

Even when it came to picking classes my mother emphasized balance over rigor. Like many international schools UNIS had the International Baccalaureate (IB). The IB curriculum started in the mid-1960s in international schools to enable children of expats to attend university in their home country. It has since gained recognition and respect from the world's leading universities. Being a teacher at UNIS, my mother was well aware of how rigorous and stressful this program could be. It was optional

[33] Goleman, Daniel, *Emotional Intelligence: Why It Can Matter More Than IQ,* (New York, Bantam Books, 1995).

at the school so while she was extremely supportive of our doing the IB she would advise us to do it in a balanced way to avoid what she considered unnecessary pressure.

"No need to pick all the hardest subjects as the IBH[34] classes. You already have Higher Physics, why do you need to do Higher Math also? Why not balance it with IBH Art? In years to come it's not going to matter that you did IBH for all the subjects that were the hardest for you. In the end they just average your grades across all your courses. Save yourself some stress and also include subjects where you have a natural advantage."

My mother had similar advice when I was at Yale. "If you're going to take Econometrics, balance that with Art History instead of another quantitative course that will just be stressful for you. You're not planning to be an economist and being able to talk about the Renaissance and Neoclassicism will come in handy." She was right again.[35]

---

[34] IBH meant Higher Level classes.

[35] This advice is actually something I remind myself about now. I have a tendency to want to go for the job perceived as the hardest. Instead of playing to my strengths, I can end up revealing my weaknesses. When I was just starting out my career this approach worked fine. It was a good thing to try to round out various skill sets. I had a natural proclivity toward marketing and communications so I went out of my way to take some assignments in finance and risk. At some point, however, I've learned that in order to continue succeeding you need to start focusing on what you're good at. You'll save yourself some stress and have more balance in your life as a result.

Senior year at UNIS (1994)

PERSONAL DEVELOPMENT

*W*hen *my family first moved to New York City* I turned into a shell of my former self. Nothing—not even the best coming-of-age films at that time—would have prepared me for the move to New York at the awkward age of 11 going on 12. In my mind, it was going to be the best year of my life in Vancouver (thanks to JAM, my soon-to-be status as a seventh grader—the last year of elementary school in Canada—and the fact that I was one of the more popular kids in my class of 25). But alas, my mother secured a teaching job at UNIS, and I never got to experience the peak of social life in Vancouver. Instead, I entered this crazy world where students French kissed in the hallways, used a ton of swear words and smoked cigarettes. Oh, and everyone's parents seemed to be divorced.[36] I was not in Our Lady of Lourdes anymore. I thought I was a darn good dresser back in Vancouver, but my clothes seemed lame in New York. I felt pretty cute strutting my

---

[36] In retrospect, it was probably just a fraction of kids who did these things, but the number was magnified in my head as I had never seen such actions in real life before except on TV in after school specials.

stuff around Coquitlam but at UNIS I was practically invisible. Recess breaks were never long enough for me in the past, but now I spent them in a bathroom stall waiting for time to pass.

My mother tried everything to make me more comfortable in my new surroundings. She befriended Arlene, the middle school guidance counselor, who promised to look out for me after I spent half of my first day lost every time the bell rang (the whole moving classrooms thing was new for me since my entire school life before then had been in one homeroom where you had the same teacher for every subject except music and gym). She approached colleagues who had children in my grade to help me make friends. She also solicited help from Benjamin (BJ) Centenera, family friend and school heartthrob. BJ was the youngest son of Tita Tessie (aka Mrs. Centenera) who was a third grade teacher at UNIS and former colleague of my mother's at International School Manila. My mother and Tita Tessie had stayed in touch since working together in the Philippines. It was she who had told my mother about the job opening at UNIS and encouraged her to apply. Before meeting Tita Tessie, I thought I might have negative associations with her since I held her largely responsible for our move. Once we met, however, it was hard not to warm up to her. She went out of her way to make the transition as smooth as possible for our family even driving us to and from school insisting it was on her way in from New Jersey.

BJ was a senior in high school and little did I know his status and influence. On our rides to and from school every day, he would ask me and Justin how we liked UNIS so far. Justin's response was always more enthusiastic. Apparently making friends in the third grade was easy. I would try to feign excitement but BJ could see through it. "Still getting used to it, huh? Don't worry, it just takes some time," he would say as he tousled my hair and messed up the bangs that had taken 15 minutes to blow dry.

One recess as I was pretending to be engrossed in arranging books in my locker, I heard a familiar voice coming down the crowded hallway. "Hey, little sis! How's it going?" It was BJ standing over me. Suddenly I could feel all eyes around me watching. "So what time are we going home today?" I don't even know if I answered him. All I remember is a flock of girls who came running up to me the minute he turned the corner. *"Hi! What's your name again? You're new here, right? So how do you know BJ?"* It was May Oishi, one of the popular girls. I still remember her green Gap pocket T, matching socks and white Keds. "We should hang out sometime," she continued. I knew BJ was just trying to help facilitate friendships on my behalf but it aggravated me even more that kids who otherwise paid no attention to me now suddenly wanted to be friends. I didn't take the bait and instead walked away, quietly leaving BJ's efforts in vain.[37]

My mother often recalls how uncharacteristically frequent I had a "long face" when we first moved to the city. She observed my insecurities grow and my confidence fade. At least while I was in New York. Once I got back to Vancouver the old Claire was back. The first summer after moving away our classes finished on June 20th and I begged my parents to book my flight back to Vancouver on June 21st. I would spend all summer in my comfort zone and come back Labor Day Weekend just in time to start school. Red

On the UNIS rooftop during our ten year high school reunion (2008)

---

[37] May and I eventually did end up becoming friends and we still laugh about her sudden interest in me when she realized I was BJ's "little sis." She and Alexis Neophytides became my closest friends from UNIS and 20 years later both were bridesmaids at my wedding in the Philippines.

flags went up for my parents as they heard me say things like, "I guess I can be OK with ¼ of the year in Vancouver. My time in New York I'll just be in school anyway. As long as I can keep going back to Vancouver I won't have to worry about making too many friends here... ." To this day Justin still teases me about a letter of mine to Henny that he found saying something deeply poignant like, "They may call New York 'The Big Apple' but Vancouver will always be 'The Big Mango' and you know how much more I like mangoes."

This was the only time in my life when I spent more hours writing than socializing. It was before email and even fax machines. I must have written a couple of letters each night and the highlight of everyday was getting home to check the mailbox. Henny's letters were most frequent but I also corresponded regularly with all my former classmates from Our Lady of Lourdes. My mother still recalls Leila's sketch of the seating chart of the seventh grade class. Leila knew these details were important to me. At the start of every school year we would anxiously wait to find out where our desks were located. Were they close to the front? Close to each other? Close to Joy? Stacy? Jonathan? Denis? Who was in front of us, behind us, to our left, to our right? It sounds funny now but hey, you were stuck in those seats for six hours every day for the next 10 months. Seating assignments could make or break your year.

I often think about how much I would have used Facebook, WhatsApp, Skype and all the other digital communication tools if these had been available then. It could have saved me boatloads of tears during those first two lonely years but I would have sorely missed the experience of writing as much as I did. When I wasn't writing letters I was writing books. Yes, books. I would rigorously draft page after page on those Mead Composition notebooks (of the black marble variety) sometimes filling out 100 college ruled sheets in the course of an evening. Don't get me wrong, I wasn't coming up with the next Pulitzer Prize winner or anything. My book series was called Marc Crescent Meadows and it was heavily inspired by teen novel series Sweet Valley High (thank you, Francine Pascal). Marc Crescent was the street on which my cousins lived and it was the most elegant sounding name I had ever heard. The books followed the lives of four best friends in high school: Alyssa Johnson (named after Alyssa Milano from *Who's the Boss?*[38]), Amanda Rogers, Caitlin Brewington and Theresa Thomson. It was like I was trying to write a spin-off about the friends of Elizabeth and Jessica Wakefield.[39]

My mother was impressed by my prolific writing though concerned about my social well-being. It was atypical for me to do things like plead not to go to sleepover camp. Part of the UNIS middle school curriculum included a week away at Camp Mason (the city kids needed to get some outdoor experience). I remember writing a letter to Leila expressing how I would have given anything to have a camp week back at Our Lady of Lourdes. "It would have been so much fun with all of our Lourdes friends but it's just the opposite here."

My mother wanted me to have the same Vancouver confidence everywhere. Not just in my small pond. The second summer I was back in Vancouver she enrolled me in a "personal development" course at John Casablancas Modeling and Career Center established by the founder of Elite modeling agency. There are conflicting opinions about John Casablancas and his self-proclaimed career centers. Some say it's a con that preys on the dreams of star struck kids and parents. Others profess it has helped them launch their modeling and acting careers. And then there are those like my mother who claim that it helps children by elevating their self-esteem, with many parents speaking about how confident their children became after completing the training.

She put me in the course not because she had grand plans for me to become a model. She thought it could help me gain

---

[38] You guessed it—another '80s TV sitcom. This one starred Tony Danza who played a retired baseball player who moves to Connecticut to work as a housekeeper so he can give his daughter a better life. Alyssa Milano played his daughter, and she quickly became one of the most popular teen idols.

[39] Elizabeth and Jessica Wakefield were the 16-year-old twin protagonists in *Sweet Valley High*.

confidence in any setting. She was from an era when charm school wasn't a punch line but rather a conventional path. Enrolling me in a class like this one after noticing my wallflower transformation seemed like a reasonable plan of action. It was certainly an investment because a personal development course at John Casablancas came with a price tag. For my mother to commit to that kind of expense makes me realize I must have been quite the sad case when we moved to New York. She justified the cost to my father by rationalizing that they had put thousands of dollars aside for my piano and violin lessons so I could be well-rounded but a strong sense of self was even more critical for a balanced child. My father agreed. Of course, it didn't hurt that my Lola Ely was going to subsidize the course as part of her birthday present to me.

My mother was constantly coming up with plans that could benefit as many people as possible. In this case, she had worked out an arrangement where my Lola could bring me to class in the city every morning and then go to Mass at the Cathedral, conveniently located across the street from John Casablancas. Lola would feel needed, Claire would feel more confident. Lola would have an outing every day, Claire would have a way to get downtown. Indeed, it was a win-win but more importantly it

John Casablancas headshot (1990)

turned out to be a very special time together for the two of us. The bus ride to town from Coquitlam took nearly an hour so it was a good chance for us to exchange stories. Lola took pleasure in hearing about all the attention I was getting during my summer homecoming, and I enjoyed getting her feisty input ("If so-and-so really wants to see you they will offer to come pick you up in Coquitlam"). Decades later my Lola would still fondly recall our daily commutes that summer.

I came back to New York the following fall ready to turn over a new leaf. It was partly John Casablancas and partly a number of other factors. I finally realized I needed to make friends and adjust to life in New York. Also, a new flock of students including Alexis Neophytides (the daughter of my mother's doctor) joined UNIS for high school, shaking up the middle school social hierarchy. Alexis was exactly the type of person you wanted to enter the scene. Not only was she strikingly pretty, she was also remarkably nice—to everyone. All the cliques welcomed her with open arms and since she was so inclusive it started to feel as though the rest of us were accepted too. I don't think she put too much thought into it (she was just being herself and she'll probably laugh when she reads this) but whatever the case it certainly benefited the

Surprise birthday party with UNIS friends (1992)

greater student body. I started holding my head high walking down the hallways (even past the cool kids' lockers). I didn't go all out and do the runway walk that I learned at John Casablancas but I developed good posture and that alone gave me more "presence." I still wore most of the clothes I had before the summer but I must have worn them with more confidence after because everyone including the popular girls started complimenting me on my wardrobe (and even asking to borrow some pieces—a common practice back in high school equivalent to the biggest form of flattery). I started feeling comfortable talking to anyone regardless of grade, clique or gender. Today my husband and brother often tease me about being overly confident. "One notch down," Justin will say implying I need to be more humble. The first time Alex was around as we recounted the early days in New York and the John Casablancas course he joked, "That's how you got like this? You should be giving back to that school's alumni fund!"

Personal development is not to be underrated. I've seen it manifest itself in so many ways. My parents are total opposites, and sometimes I wonder how they ended up together. The unromantic version of their courtship includes my mother trying to dodge a *Single White Female* type,[40] my mother avoiding being a spinster, my mother ready to move out of her parents' house, you get the gist. But the times I have heard the "romantic" version of the story it involves my mother describing how impressed she was by my father's natural ability to talk to anyone whether it was her stern father or the house maid, the principal of her school or the maintenance man. It's actually a quality I consider my mother to equally possess but she reminds me that she was a late bloomer and this characteristic only developed over time.

---

[40] *Single White Female* reference is based on a 1992 thriller film in which a young woman literally tries to become her successful roommate. It has since come to be used interchangeably with "stalker."

Back then, when my mother would have us come to her classroom to attend a special event or school program, I didn't realize it was intentional. I figured she wanted Justin and me to help pass around food or assist with cleanup, but the main reason she insisted we come was to expose us to different people. The UNIS parents were an impressively diverse bunch and it became routine for us to chat up the President of the Guggenheim Museum one minute and the Upper West Side stay-at-home mom the next. As we helped my mother host her classroom parents year after year, we became increasingly more comfortable talking to anyone. It turns out to be a skill that comes in handy during so many instances whether meeting your boyfriend's parents for the first time, charming the pants off everyone at a corporate dinner or trying to get an upgrade on a flight. My mother was well aware of this advantage and leveraged every opportunity for her children to develop this competence, often without us noticing.

May at I at UN General Assembly (1994)

Trying on the bridesmaid dresses that May designed for her wedding (2006)

Annual UNIS-UN Conference (1994)

The night of my mom's UNIS retirement party with Tita Tessie and Tito Centy (2006)

In front of May's workplace on Rivington Street in the East Village (2006)

Alexis delivering her speech at our UNIS graduation—behind her is former Secretary General Kofi Annan (1994)

Shamelessly karaoking in front of my UNIS classmates (1992)

Harvard-Yale Weekend in New Haven (1997)

My girlfriends Melissa, May and Kristen at Duane Reade, our favorite meeting spot in the evenings as someone was always late and the early ones could read magazines or browse through cosmetic products while waiting (2005)

Alexis and I visiting actress and former Yale classmate Kellie Martin in LA (2005)

New Year's Eve with my best friend from childhood, Henny, and my best friend from college, Kristen (2005)

Alex and I in Sao Paulo (2006)

*B*alancing personal and professional priorities is an ongoing challenge for many people and one that my mother has always helped me with. When I was nearing the end of my management program and deciding whether to stay in Brazil or go to the Philippines I was initially just thinking about what assignment would be perceived as more challenging. Brazil was one of our "hypergrowth" markets so it meant more exposure and higher profile projects plus it was still a relatively new country experience for me. The Philippines was a smaller market, not considered "priority" at the time and it was a place with which I was already familiar. My mother would remind me about other factors to consider, mainly that both my grandmothers living in Manila were nearing their 90s and the chance to spend time with them could be an unexpected gift (plus the idea of me being based in the Philippines as an expat would give them so much bragging rights). Both of my grandfathers had passed away decades earlier so we tried not to take for granted the precious time with our living grandmothers.

I weighed everything out. I had already spent six months in Brazil during which time I had managed to build a strong network there. After my six months in the Philippines I could go back to Brazil for a permanent role if I wanted whereas the opportunity to spend time with my grandmothers may never come again. I decided to go to Manila and it was one of the best decisions I have made. It turned out to be an invaluable work experience as I was able to build a new business model by leveraging the growing call center business in the Philippines. More importantly, I had quality time with each of my grandmothers before they passed away.

I was always very close to my maternal grandmother, Lola Ely. My cousins would often tease that I was her favorite and I embraced the role wholeheartedly. I was also the only grandchild being raised outside the Philippines so even though she and Lolo Seny already had six *apos*[41], I was the first baby they ever experienced hands on (read: no *yaya*[42]). In the Philippines there would have been someone dedicated to looking after my every need as a baby. Her sole purpose would be to rock me to sleep, feed me, change me and even watch me sleep. I've often heard people say that the only time many parents in the Philippines see their baby is when the baby is calm, clean and fed. For our family in Canada, this arrangement was not the case. My parents had to care for me with no assistance and my grandparents who made the long trip from the Philippines to see their grandchild had to do the same. My mother often recalls what a memorable sight it was for her to come home and see my Lola rocking me humming the *tinikling*[43] song as she tried to stop my fussing.

---

[41] *Apô* means "grandchild."

[42] *Yayá* means "nanny."

[43] The *tinikling* dance is one of the most popular and well-known of traditional Philippine dances. It is a pre-Spanish dance that involves two people beating, tapping, and sliding bamboo poles on the ground and against each other in coordination with one or more dancers who step over and in between the poles in a dance.

My parents and grandparents (1974)

Lola Ely, Mom and me (1978)

We were bonded from the beginning and I always felt special to her. She would love how I imitated her nighttime routine in front of the mirror ending with the final application of Oil of Olay. She would listen to my stories from school and be the first to call anyone who remotely crossed me a "snake in the grass." She would continuously brag about me even in my presence, "She's a Yale scholar, you know…" And sometimes her compliments would make me a little embarrassed, "She's even prettier than this but she likes to tan."[44] Lola Ely passed away the year after I left the Philippines and I'm so grateful to have been able to spend the last year of her life with her.

My relationship with my paternal grandmother, Lola Adoring, was a little different. She and my Lolo Toni already had 10 *apos* by the time I came around so I didn't feel particularly special as far as grandchildren were concerned. In fact, quite the opposite. My father's only sister, Nori, had married a young Iraqi named Riadh whom she met through my dad. He and Tito Riadh (as we have always called him) were classmates at the American

---

[44] We always chalked up these types of comments to "colonial mentality."

Framed photos of Tito Riadh's father and Tita Nori's father (my Lolo Toni) that I will always associate with my cousins' home

University in Cairo. Lolo Toni was working for the Philippines' Department of Foreign Affairs and he had been assigned to Egypt in the late '60s so most of the family had relocated there. My father and Tito Riadh became good friends quickly and my father started inviting him over to the house regularly. Most of Tito Riadh's family was in Baghdad and because of political reasons he could not return there. Soon enough he became an unofficial member of the Lim household having dinner with the family during the week and playing mahjong with them on weekends. I later learned that Tito Riadh's father was a major general in the opposition party in Iraq and Saddam Hussein was charging him with spying for Americans. The Lims followed the trial over the radio with Tito Riadh and they were with him when he learned that his father was being sentenced to public execution. This would cross my mind years down the line when Tito Riadh was actively speaking out against the American invasion of Iraq. At the time there were many arguing that the US would be helping the Iraqi people by bringing down Saddam Hussein. I remember thinking that if anyone would want the removal of Saddam Hussein it would be Tito Riadh. It spoke volumes to me that despite all the appalling actions by the dictator Tito Riadh and many Iraqis like him were protesting American intervention.

Lolo Toni with President Sukarno of Indonesia and President Ayub Khan in Pakistan (1963)

My father's family and Tito Riadh became even closer and four years later he opened up to my dad about his feelings for Tita Nori. Eventually they married and had three adorable *mestizo*[45] children, Natasha, Faisal and Walid. Anyone even vaguely familiar with the Philippines knows about the premium placed on being mixed (with Caucasian genes), thanks to the colonial mentality that has been engrained into society. Even at a young age I could understand that my cousin Natasha would likely be my Lola Adoring's favorite. Not only was she the only daughter of her only daughter, but she was also a beautiful little girl (with doll- like almond shaped eyes and chestnut brown hair) with a charming personality.

It wasn't until my time working in the Philippines that I realized how close I could become to Lola Adoring. I bonded with her more during my six months in the Philippines than I had in my 29 years. At the age of 90, Lola Adoring was still extremely "with it." I would sit in the room with her for hours going through pictures and for the first time truly appreciating the rich life she and my Lolo had experienced. Lolo Toni ended his career as a Consul General for the Philippines and his work had taken his

---

[45] *Mêstizo* is a term traditionally used in Spain, Latin America and the Philippines for people mixed descent.

Lolo Toni and family meeting Pope Paul VI (1971)

family to Seoul, Karachi and Rome in addition to Cairo. They had photos with everyone from various heads of states to Pope Paul VI. When we weren't in her room looking at albums, she would come out with us for a night of ballroom dancing or play mahjong with us until the wee hours. Lola Adoring didn't like to miss out on anything. Her children would offer to bring her home early if it got too late and she would always refuse. If she wasn't included in plans for a trip out of concern that the journey would be hazardous she would insist on going anyway. My friends would always tease me about my fear of missing out[46] and after spending time with Lola Adoring it became very evident where I got it. I'm still the last to go to bed when I have cousins or friends staying over, I never let myself fall asleep on a road trip because I don't want to miss out on conversation and I hate to leave any party early. Missing out on this time with Lola Adoring would have been one of my biggest regrets.

---

[46] The new word for this is "FOMO."

My cousins in front of their sari-sari store in Quezon City (2006)

With my dad's brother Tito Eddie and Lola Adoring during a night of ballroom dancing (2006)

Lolo Ely and Lolo Seny (1940)

Hosting friends during my assignment in Brazil (2005)

Campaigning for Hillary Clinton (2008)

I WANT TO BE PRESIDENT

O*ne of the benefits of going to a school like Yale* is the peer pressure to aim high. "I want to be President" is not just something cute you remember your kindergarten classmates reciting at an elementary school program. The concept is alive and well on Ivy League campuses though stated with more subtlety. "I have some political aspirations," your roommate may say coyly. Everything is within reach, and nothing is unattainable. Whether you took a job with a Wall Street firm, Teach for America, or Senator Schumer, the plan is to be at the very top. Upon graduation from college there was a big emphasis on setting ourselves up for professional success. While many children of our family friends were starting to marry and settle down in their mid-20s most of my college peers were heavily focused on careers, i.e., getting into the right law school, getting tapped for the right leadership program, working for the right judge.

My closest friends from Yale were prime examples:

- Sheldon was teaching himself to program so he could develop an algorithm to predict consumer behavior online[47]
- Danny was pursuing a JD/MBA while working full-time as a lobbyist and campaigning for Democratic nominee John Kerry in Washington, DC
- Khamen was opening his own sports medicine practice[48] across the country after finishing his medical residency at Mount Sinai
- Kristen was completing the Root-Tilden-Kern Program, the nation's premier public service scholarship, at NYU Law
- Bianca was about to make partner at the venerable Los Angeles talent firm Gang Tyre (home of such legends as Steven Spielberg and Clint Eastwood)
- Tanya was completing the prestigious Yale-China Teaching Fellowship at The Chinese University of Hong Kong
- Harold was securing investors in his own investment management firm
- Nic was starting his job as a Policy Advisor for the Mayor of San Francisco
- Ken was clerking for Judge Denny Chin who presided over *US v. Madoff*[49] (President Obama later nominated Chin to the United States Court of Appeals for the Second Circuit)
- James was starting a micro-lending company to help the under-banked Hispanic community build credit[50] and being asked to speak at the Clinton Global Initiative

---

[47] After developing his algorithm, Sheldon Gilbert founded Proclivity Media, a company recognized for pioneering the new field of predictive advertising.

[48] East Valley Spine & Sports Medical Center is now one of Arizona's leading sources for treatment, rehabilitation and prevention of sports injuries.

[49] In 2008 former NASDAQ Chairman Bernard Madoff admitted that the wealth management arm of his business was an elaborate Ponzi scheme.

[50] Progreso Financiero, founded by James Gutierrez, went on to make over 250,000 loans through 83 locations in California and Texas.

Marriage and starting a family were not top of mind at the time. As the cliché goes, we were about working hard and playing hard (and networking in between). Last year I came across an article called "Friends of a Certain Age"[51] that reminded me how lucky I am to have met these friends when I did. The writer, Alex Williams, describes how, no matter how many friends you make in your 30s and 40s through work, children's play dates, and Facebook, none will come close to the kind you made in college when you had proximity, repeated unplanned interactions and a setting that encouraged people to let their guard down. As you get older, schedules get tight, family obligations increase and priorities change, which make it harder to make actual close friends—the kind you call in a crisis. "It's time to resign yourself to situational friends," Williams sums up.

It's an extreme conclusion and I would be the first to argue that great friends can most certainly be made post-college based on my own experience. That said, I do agree it's hard to replicate those relationships built on a foundation of consecutive nights ending with breakfast at a diner and brunches that turn into dinners that turn into drinks. This time together would be spent discussing everything from why the US shouldn't invade Iraq to what kind of party we were going to throw for 4th of July; why so-and-so will never be able to settle down with anyone to what kind of business we should be investing in together; why we should be supporting a certain political candidate to what kind of fundraising event we should organize for the Tsunami victims. Just being around each other provided positive energy and encouragement. Not to mention fun.

My parents were extremely supportive of my pursuing opportunities in different parts of the world (not exactly conducive to settling down), and they didn't bat an eyelid when my long-term relationship (on path to marriage) ended abruptly just as

[51] Williams, Alex (2012, July 13). Friends of a Certain Age. *The New York Times*. Retrieved from http://www.nytimes.com.

so many of their friends' children were walking down the aisle. People would comment, "You must be feeling some pressure from your parents to meet someone." No, actually, I wasn't.

Not until the year I turned 30 and met Alex did my  mother make any comment in this regard. It was after I finished my assignment in the Philippines and was deciding whether to go back to Brazil, stay on in the Philippines or return to New York. Most of my colleagues in the program continued working abroad (it was considered the faster path to running a business since many of these roles were in emerging markets where one had the opportunity to take on a relatively big job, the equivalent of which would not be available in global headquarters).

The guys at Khamen and Yara's wedding in Puerto Rico (2006)

"At this point in your life it's OK to let a 'friend' factor into your decision," she would say. (My parents never used the term "boyfriend." It could be a "close" friend or a "special" friend but in their minds nothing was official until marriage, so why give anything in between a title.) She continued, "You've put a lot of focus on your career, which is great, so now you can balance it by putting some attention on other important things." After our assignments had finished in Brazil, Alex went back to New York and I went to the Philippines. We left more as friends than anything else but soon found ourselves staying in close touch while on opposite sides of the globe. We spoke at least two times a day despite the time difference, and he even came out to see me in Manila. I decided to take a job back in New York and see where the relationship could go.

Balance can be applied to everything from wardrobe to food regimen to career. If you're wearing a short mini, keep the

In Miami with good friends Ben, Carmela and Sheldon (2005)

Some of the Yale crew. From left to right: Sheldon, Bianca, Danny, me, Alex, Yara, Khamen, Kristen (2009)

top blousy. If you had a salad for lunch, enjoy dessert after dinner. After the dense *Economist* read, indulge in some light *Us Weekly*. If you've splurged on a lavish party or night out for yourself, contribute generously to a cause that helps others. If you've spent years plotting out your education and professional track, take some time to think about your personal life.

Kristen and I at the Democratic National Convention in Denver (2008)

My 29th birthday dinner when I was back from Brazil for two days. Top row left to right: Kristen, Mom, May, Justin. Bottom row left to right: Khamen, me, Danny (2005)

With Bianca, James and Kristen at the DNC after party (2008)

View from my Durfee Hall dorm room on Yale's Old Campus (1994)

Post brunch drinks with Kristen, Danny and Ken (2006)

Our favorite pastime—picnicking in Central Park (2007)

With my Yale
Class of '98 crew
during Harvard-
Yale weekend
senior year (1997)

No one was more excited than our family about Costco's NYC opening in Harlem (2009)

IMMIGRANT PARENT
PLAYBOOK

YAKKETY YAK

*I*t could be a totally unfounded hypothesis but I've often seen a direct correlation between how much immigrant parents were assimilated, i.e., "Americanized" and how much their kids talked back. Fresh off the boat, most well-behaved kids. Abroad longer and more "Americanized," mouthy, sometimes disrespectful, kids. It's a sweeping generalization—not to say all American kids are disrespectful to their parents—but it's been my broad observation.

I remember watching an episode of the *Brady Bunch* when Marcia Brady was so upset with her parents that she stormed out of the room and slammed her bedroom door. It sounds silly but I remember admiring the way her long hair swung around as she made her dramatic exit. I wanted to try it one day. The opportunity presented itself shortly after when my mother was scolding me for not cleaning up my room as I had promised. This was my first and last attempt at the Marcia Brady storm out/hair flip because my mother did not find it remotely cute. She took it as a huge sign of disrespect and immediately nipped this practice in the bud. And it wasn't only about storming out. If she even caught a glimpse of us

Freshman suitemates (1994)

starting to roll our eyes, she didn't let it pass. "Don't give me that exasperated look. I'm your mother, not one of your friends."

My mother was extremely warm with us but she often made clear the distinction between parents and friends. For instance, when she would criticize something we did and detect that we didn't want to hear anymore she'd say, "I'm telling you because I'm your mother and no one cares more than me. Otherwise, who's going to tell you... [fill in the blank with closest friend at the time]?" For my brother, it was Nadeen. She was Justin's best friend from third grade all the way through high school.

"Who's going to tell you... Nadeen?" my mother would say at the airport after telling Justin he should speak louder so the immigration officer could hear him.

"Who's going to tell you... Nadeen?" she would say

another time after reminding him to look someone in the eyes while shaking hands.

"Who's going to tell you?" became a running joke in the family when one day eight- year-old Justin started answering the rhetorical question with a small sigh, "Nadeen..."

When I first got to Yale, I quickly learned that I needed to get a little more assertive if I ever wanted to be heard. Not just in the classroom but in the dorm room. My naturally pleasant Filipino-Canadian-New York-but-United Nations-educated approach was not conducive to holding my own when it came to reasoning with former debate team captain type roommates and dorm neighbors about everything from who should have the bigger room to whether or not God exists. It took some time but by Thanksgiving break I had developed my own signature assertive (sometimes condescendingly argumentative) tone that seemed to work with everyone. Everyone but my mother, that is. Who would have guessed that she wouldn't appreciate being spoken to like an 18-year-old freshman? The first time I used it on her she gave me that stern look of hers and it was like I had tried the Marcia Brady hair flip again.

"My case is based on universally agreed upon premises. What's the basis for your argument?" I had asked.

"The basis is I'm your mother. That tone may work with your classmates at Yale but you will never win that way with me." Once again, if my mother perceived any sign of disrespect she put a stop to it immediately. That's when I learned that as important as it is to acquire an aggressive tone, equally essential is knowing when to use it.

Certain actions may seem insignificant and inconsequential at first but they can make a difference in the long run because they build positive behavioral qualities early on. Here are a few that come to mind:

1. Use Tito, Tita, Uncle, Auntie or some form of respect before the first name of those a generation or more older. I realize there are some cultures (or social circles) where

this isn't common practice but generally speaking I think it's the better default when addressing elders.

2. Greet properly. When we were kids and our parents got home, we would stop whatever it was we were doing to go up and give them a kiss and a proper greeting. Saying hi from where we were sitting on the couch just wouldn't cut it.

3. Insist your children tell their friends they need to greet you properly too.

4. Never let your children get away with mouthing off and storming out of the room. As parents, you should decide when the conversation is over.

5. Insist your children sit in the front seat while you're driving them and their friends around. It's normal for them to want to sit in the back with their peers but they should sit up front with you out of respect. You're not their driver.

There are also particular words that fall into the category of seemingly harmless until put into practice. Growing up I thought it was a little strange that we weren't allowed to say any derivation of the word "bored." We'd hear other kids say it all the time and it didn't seem to be a bad word. The first time I said, "I'm bored" to my mother she responded with, "You're too smart and creative to be bored. Use your imagination and entertain yourself." She was right. We were kids. We could always find something to keep us amused even if it was daring one another to sneak into the kitchen of someone's house we were visiting to grab a Pringle from on top of the fridge.[52]

---

[52] Pringles were one of those food items we didn't have very often as kids. Not because it was considered unhealthy or anything but because it was more expensive than your regular bag of chips. It fell into the same category as After Eights chocolate mints. We never had it in our kitchen so we'd get excited anytime we'd see it at someone else's home.

Now I understand why she didn't want the word in our vernacular. Once a kid gets in the habit of saying something is "boring" they are quick to overuse it, often doing so in a setting that will offend someone or at least put them on the defensive. "I'm bored..." The host will feel compelled to come over, "Does he want to watch TV in the bedroom?"

Recently we had dinner out with friends who had their niece in town. She was 12 years old, and her parents had left her with our friends (her aunt and uncle) for a week while they took an anniversary trip to Europe. She seemed like a cute kid, and I could tell from the conversation that she was widely entertained that week in the best places (Singapore Zoo, Universal Studios, Singapore Flyer) and restaurants (all-you-can-eat Japanese, Din Tai Fung, Osteria Mozza). While we were waiting for dessert my friend turned to her and asked, "What are you thinking over there?" She responded, "Nothing. I'm bored. Simple as that." All of a sudden the cute kid seemed spoiled and ungrateful.

Other words that fall into this category:

- Stupid: Only adults (and only some adults) should be qualified to use this word. Little kids just sound like know-it-alls.
- Hate: Too much of a negative word. Children haven't seen or experienced enough of the world to know what hate means
- Shut up: Another "bratty" expression to be avoided for as long as possible.

Dad helping me drive my stuff to and from Miami (2005)

GOOD COP, BAD COP

My parents did many things well but they were particularly impressive when it came to good cop, bad cop. They could play either role masterfully depending on the situation. When it came to manners, being respectful, overall behavior and the proper way of doing things, my mother was police chief. When it came to going out during the teen years especially if both genders were in attendance my father was police commissioner.

It would be especially intimidating to me because my father is otherwise the most laid back and easygoing guy. He never gets embarrassed so he is always happy to put himself out there to break the ice (or for no reason at all). He'll be first on the dance floor at a wedding reception (even if he's not attending but just happens to be walking by), he has no qualms about putting on a piano performance in a crowded hotel lobby lounge (even if he doesn't know how to play) and he'll carry on a conversation with the non-English speaking taxi driver in Cuba (even when he doesn't speak a lick of Spanish).

It is hard then to imagine this same individual not so much as crack a smile when some of my friends would cheerfully greet him. My father would drop me off and pick me up every time I had a party or event in high school. Sometimes I would ask if we could give one of my friends a lift home. He always agreed, but he would transform into this stern Asian man once my friends entered the car.

"Thanks so much, Mr. Lim! It's super cold so I really appreciate the ride... Anyway, it's so nice to see you again. How are you and Mrs. Lim?" my friend May would say in her bubbly voice.

"Welcome. Fine," he would curtly respond. There goes my strangely quiet and stern Asian father again. *Who is this man?* I would think. I wanted my friends to see how funny and cool my dad was.

"Hey Dad," I would try to get the fun out of him, "did you perfect the Michael Jackson song? May, my dad loves the *Black and White* video. He can do all the—"

"No," my father would cut me off and the rest of the ride would be in silence.

After a few more stern Asian man experiences with my dad, I asked my mother what the deal was. Why couldn't he be more like the dads on TV who were so friendly with their kids' friends? I could picture Mr. Keaton asking Skippy how his day was or Dr. Huxtable teasing one of Vanessa's friends.[53] I knew he had it in him. That's how he was with my cousins after all.

"Just let it be," my mother would tell me. "I can be the nice one with your friends. It's good they're not too comfortable with both of us."

I didn't really understand what she meant at the time, but years later my father became his normal self around my friends. We would all be together attending one of my mother's art shows and I would find my dad going out of his way to chat with May and Alexis. At one point he was asking May about her new boyfriend

---

[53] More '80s TV sitcom references. This time to *Family Ties* as well as *The Cosby Show*.

and then later in the evening he and Alexis were talking about her upcoming acting audition when she would have to kiss a girl. This was not the stern Asian man.

"Dad, you never used to talk to my friends before. You were always so cold with May and Alexis and everyone," I would comment on the drive home.

"Of course, that was intentional. They were already so at ease, I didn't want them to get even more comfortable. I could already hear May saying something like, 'C'mon, Mr. Lim. *Pleeeeease* can Claire come?' It was better for your teenage friends to be a little on edge around me. There would be plenty of time to be friendly later."

I relayed this strategy to May who had the same light bulb go off, "Wow! It totally worked. When you were around I wouldn't dare do anything that might get us in trouble because I was scared of your dad. Man, they're good!"

My father also had this knack for knowing exactly how to rain on my parade when it came to boys during my early teen years. During my summers in Vancouver the place to see and be seen was the PNE. The Pacific National Exhibition (as no one called it) was the annual 18-day summer fair that started in 1910 as a showcase of British Columbia to the rest of Canada and the world. At one point it was said to be the second largest event of its kind in North America behind only the New York State Fair. In my adolescent world the PNE was synonymous with youthful summers and coming of age. Everyone who was anyone got some kind of job at the fair, whether it was taking tickets for rides in Playland, swirling cotton candy at the snack stands or even working as a sweeper. In our case my parents partnered with friends to put up a Filipino food booth called *Philippine Carinderia* and working there was a rite of passage for every one of my cousins and peers. My best friend Henny's oldest sister, Amy, was one of the first. Next

Philippine Carinderia at the PNE (1983)

Justin and I making deliveries at the PNE (1984)

was her middle sister, Bet. Then my cousin Natasha. Henny and I anxiously awaited the day we were old enough to work on the frontline (12 was sufficient). Of course, it wasn't the idea of serving *pancit*, *lumpia* and *pork bbq*[54] that got us excited about our first job but rather the access (and attention) we would get by being center stage at the place to be.

Our enthusiasm was dampened, however, when my father's schedule showed that we would work on alternate days: Henny on Monday and Wednesday, I on Tuesday and Thursday, etc. Our hearts had been set on working together. I don't know why we assumed we would have this privilege since everyone before us had worked on his or her own. But no one else was attached at the hip the way we were so we assumed everyone knew we came as a pair. When it was explained to us that the budget didn't allow for two people to be working the front of the booth Henny and I quickly

---

[54] Filipino staple foods. *Pancit* refers to popular rice noodle dish, *lumpia* to our version of eggrolls. Pork bbq is not unique to the Philippines but let's just say we have our very special secret sauce that makes it one of a kind.

volunteered to split the $4/hour wage. We couldn't care less about the money. This gig was about a free pass to be at the PNE every day. The $2 salary was just icing on the cake. We opened up the booth at 9:00 a.m. and the fair didn't close until past midnight. Under normal circumstances my parents would never let me hang out at a summer fair every day for hours upon hours but the PNE was like a home away from home with family headquarters being the *Philippine Carinderia*.

Weeks before the PNE opened its doors, Henny and I already had our outfits planned for the two and a half weeks. During the summer months we would spend so much time together that we started to look alike. Granted, it probably had everything to do with our hair, our clothes and our makeup but whatever the case we loved the attention because people everywhere would stop us on the street to ask if we were twins.[55] We played it up shamelessly, creating matching outfits from our combined wardrobe including the clothes that were borrowed from the closets of Henny's sisters.

Coca Cola photo shoot (1990)

Henny and her sisters were young fashionistas. They would be on top of all the latest trends, often designing their own clothes that Lola Rebodos[56] would sew (she was an expert). One year we even planned a photo shoot and had my cousin Arvi take pictures of us in our twin ensembles posing with Coca Cola products. What more, we actually submitted the pictures to the Coca Cola

---

[55] We reveled in this comment because we had a mild obsession with twins. I think it was perpetuated by *Double Trouble*, *Sweet Valley High* and all the other television and book series about twins.

[56] Lola Rebodos was Henny's Lola.

Company. Well, we walked over to the Coca Cola building on Fifth Avenue and gave them to the company rep anyway. (OK, it could have been the security guy sitting in the lobby. What did we know? We were two 14-year-old girls who thought we were going to be the next Doublemint twins.[57])

My parents watched with caution and didn't hesitate to stop us if they found the lipstick too dark or the skirts too short.

Another photo shoot location (1990)

My father, in particular, would often disapprove saying that I had enough clothes of my own to wear. It didn't stop us from trying; we just hoped he would eventually let it go. That never happened, of course. Instead, my father came up with creative ways of sending his message. On Day 2 of PNE (after he got a taste of what we were planning based on Day 1) he surprised the staff by announcing we would have uniforms. He pulled out matching green aprons that we were all going to have to wear. "What? But why? How come all of a sudden?" I was the only one in a position to protest. These would cover up the entire outfits Henny and I had planned. "These aren't so bad..." Henny tried to sound positive in front of my father but I knew she was just as dismayed. There was no convincing him and everyone in the booth put on the aprons. "OK, so this just means our hair and makeup has to be perfect," Henny would think out loud. She was in fashion crisis management mode.

Henny and I came to the PNE on Day 3 with matching hairstyles (side swept ponytails) and makeup (Revlon Rum Raisin lipstick, Max Factor Smoke liquid eyeliner and Maybelline Very

---

[57] Doublemint is a chewing gum flavor by the Wrigley Company that used twins in their advertising.

Black mascara). We were determined not to let the green aprons get in the way of our style. My father observed that we were having far too much fun "working." Teenage boys would stop by the booth and talk to us, usually starting the conversation with, "Hey, are you guys twins?" By late afternoon my father was back announcing updates to the uniform. In addition to the green aprons we would all have to wear fluorescent pink caps that he pulled out of a plastic bag. "*C'mon, Dad! No way! You can't be serious!*" I turned to Henny who couldn't help but look horrified. Not only would they cover up our hair and most of our face but they were also a fashion faux pas. No one would be caught dead in those things. Nana Flor and the rest of the staff didn't look happy either but my father was not going to budge. "If you don't want to wear the hat then you can pull all your hair back into a hairnet." And that shut me up.

My attempts to find ways around my parents' rules tended to backfire. One other example of a failed plan was when I tried to get a job working alongside May and my cousin Arvi at The Gap at Herald Square. I would stop by while the two of them were doing their shift and it looked like so much fun. Basically it was a lot of young people walking around the two floors, listening to good music and hanging out. After work, May and Arvi would invite me to go out with some of their co-workers but it was often too late in the evening for me.

"It would be so fun if you worked here too," May commented one day as she folded a stack of Flare jeans. A light bulb went off in my head, and I had flashbacks to PNE days working with a best friend. I got so excited that I brought up the idea of getting a job at dinner that night. My parents seemed open to considering it. Of course, I didn't position it as a chance to hang out with May and meet new friends but rather an opportunity to get some real work experience outside of the 18-day PNE. I promised it wouldn't affect my school work and insisted I was ready for this responsibility. Plus, I could start earning and saving my own money. "OK, let's talk to Tita Baby since your cousin is doing part-time work." Tita Baby was Arvi's mother. Perfect, I thought! I'd be hanging out at

The Gap by this time on Monday if all went according to plan.

It didn't, of course. It wasn't Arvi my parents had in mind but his older sister, Michelle. Michelle worked at Laura Ashley on 57th Street between Madison and Fifth Avenues. It was a beautiful flagship store next to Burberrys and across from Tiffany but needless to say it wasn't where my teenage peers would be hanging out.

"Maybe we can also talk to Arvi and see if they're still hiring at The Gap," I suggested.

"The Gap where Arvi works is right next to the subway. There are so many people just loitering around there hanging out," my father commented. Sounded phenomenal to me!

"Laura Ashley will be a calm and controlled environment with older and more established clientele. You'll probably even be able to practice your Japanese," my mother added.

And so, instead of spending the next year meeting new friends and hanging out with teenage boy co-workers I was selling floral printed dresses alongside middle aged female associates and practicing my foreign language skills. Damn, my parents were good.

At times friends and even family would comment that my

Trying to replicate the PNE pork BBQ experience (2009)

parents (in particular, my father) were being too strict with me. It was not uncommon for them to offer up opinions and ideas on the matter. My cousin Arvi had a friend named Jay who also worked at The Gap. Jay and I met at a family wedding. I caught the bouquet, he caught the garter belt and it was instant matchmaking from there. He starting calling and we got to know one another a little bit more over the phone. He would ask me to join him and Arvi after they got off work but as was the case with May, it was always too late for me to go. Not to mention I wasn't exactly allowed to date. My parents might approve group outings during the day or inviting friends over to our place but that was about it. My mother was empathetic as she watched me attempt to manage my teenage social life within tight parameters. She grew up under the strictest 1950s rules and while my father would be considered lenient compared to her parents she knew it was a different time and when you adjusted for decades I was probably experiencing the same thing she did. That said, she always maintained I needed to abide by my father's rules.

One day I was at Arvi's place for dinner and the topic of Jay came up. Arvi's cousin Coral and her husband, John, were also there and since Jay and I met at their wedding they were curious if anything more had transpired. "No, nothing. Claire's not allowed out long enough to see Jay," Arvi teased. He enjoyed poking at my goody two shoes ways.

"What? That's too bad. Hey, why don't you guys just tell Tito Didi that she's coming here and then invite Jay over? At least they can hang out and maybe even go to the movies since it's just down the street." I don't remember who made the initial suggestion but soon enough everyone got excited about the idea. I had to admit it sounded pretty easy to pull off and kind of tempting.

When I got home I confessed the plan to my mother. I should have known she wouldn't approve but part of me thought that if she went along it was definitely okay (otherwise I would feel guilty). Not only did my mother disapprove but she was also disturbed by the thought of this plan being discussed among Arvi and his cousins in the first place. "I know it can be hard at times but you don't want to do anything that makes your father look stupid." She continued, "Think about how it would feel if everyone else knew something about you that he didn't. It would be very hurtful. You don't want to do that to someone who does so much for you. And so what if they tease you? Is Arvi going to wake up at all hours of the night to pick you up from a party? Is Coral the one driving you all over the country to look at colleges?" (It was the same rhetorical voice she used when she would say, "Who's going to tell you... Nadeen?") She continued, "You can make mistakes and you can disappoint us but whatever happens, don't let your parents be the last to know."

The message stuck with me. Certainly the last thing I would want to do is to hurt or embarrass my parents. I never ended up following through on the plan, and Arvi continued to tease me about not being able to get out from under my parents' thumb. "When you're older, you're probably going to regret not rebelling even just a little. You might feel like you missed out on being young," he and others would say.

It has actually worked out to be quite the opposite. When I think of everything my father has done for me over the years, I am so grateful for the gift of guilt. There are plenty of stories to tell but one in particular that people find hard to believe is how my father drove down to Miami with all my belongings in tow so I could attend a weekend class in New York and still start work the following Monday. When I got assigned to a six-month stint in Miami, my father offered me the use of the family car while I was down there. The plan was for us to leave mid-week and drive down to Florida together, giving me enough time to settle in over the weekend and start work that same week. It turned out, however, that I needed to attend one final weekend session of my executive MBA course in New York, which was scheduled until 5 pm the Sunday before I started work. I realized it would put a damper on our road trip plan but before I could figure out another solution my father was already offering to drive to Miami on his own earlier that week and get me settled in. "Are you sure? Thanks, Dad," was all I could say as he started helping me pack up my boxes. He started his 22-hour drive on a Wednesday night and arrived early Friday morning in time to get the keys to my new apartment (someone had to be there to receive the rental furniture that was going to be delivered). When I arrived in Miami that Sunday evening, my father was waiting at the airport. We drove back to what would be my home for the next six months. I walked into the apartment. The boxes were unpacked. Furniture was assembled. Curtains were up. The fridge was stocked. All I needed to do was get a good night's sleep before my first day of work.

He then spent the next few days in Miami teaching me how to get around. Literally, since I didn't know how to drive. Growing up in New York City, I had no need to do so. Most people learned how to drive only when moving outside the city. I had passed the DMV test in New York about a week before my move to Miami. The plan was for my father to stay my first week there so he could help me settle into my new apartment and also help me get comfortable with driving. That Monday morning we got into the car. Over the weekend my father had already tested the route from my place in South Beach to the Citi offices in Doral. I had only been at the wheel a handful of times (mostly just in preparation for my driving test) so I was very much a student

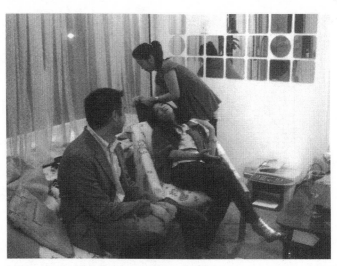

Justin and Henny visiting May at her workplace (2008)

driver. My father guided me through the roads and talked me through how to merge on the highway. Once we got to the office I went on upstairs and he drove back to the apartment (someone had to be there for the cable guy). He would drive back to Doral that evening as I was getting out of work, and my driving lesson would continue. We did this routine my entire first week. There were a couple of times I was caught off guard with my colleagues. We would be going out for lunch and my boss would say, "Claire, do you mind if we take your car? I have to take this call from New York so it would be easier if you drive." Hmm. What was the professional way of saying my car's not here because my father drives it during the day? And by the way, even though I'm almost 30, I'm not comfortable behind the wheel yet?

In addition to good cop, bad cop, below are a few other rules from the old parenting playbook that I think should still apply:

1. No entertaining in the bedroom: Somewhere between *The Cosby Show* and *Modern Family*[58] it became commonplace to watch friends of the opposite sex in the bedroom of teenage

Dad helping me pack up in Miami (2005)

---

[58] Popular American television sitcom currently on air.

kids. I don't even want to think about what Clair Huxtable would do if she found a boy in Denise or Vanessa's room. On the other hand, Claire Dunphy watches her daughter Hailey go upstairs with her boyfriend Dylan on a regular basis. Of course, I realize there are other places besides the bedroom to do certain things if kids really want to do them. But why make it easy? And why make it the norm? As crazy as it may be to think that everyone will wait until they're married to have sex, it is equally outrageous to believe that the average 14 and 15–year-old is mature enough to be having sex.

2. Keep the landline: My former Yale roommate Kristen recently blogged about how increasingly more households are getting rid of their landlines and going exclusively to cell phones.[59] For most it's a practical decision. Everyone in the family has a cell phone and no one is using the home phone anymore so why pay for the service? With the shared family phone (and before the digital age), it was easy for parents to know who their kids' friends were. There was etiquette learned from sharing the phone with your parents and siblings, properly greeting parents who answered the phone and calling (or not calling) at appropriate times. You lose these benefits when you move exclusively to cell phones.

3. Conditional sleepovers: My parents didn't believe in sleepovers as we were growing up. They would let me stay at the house of the slumber party host past midnight but they would come pick me up when things started to wind down and everyone was going to sleep. Or they would suggest we host a sleepover if I really wanted the experience. The no sleepover thing came across as

---

[59] Kristen Stiefel's insightfult blog is called *Motherese* and the piece I'm referencing is "Don't Call Us; We'll Call You."

unreasonable to most of my classmates but it was quite standard for all of our Filipino family friends, which is why I don't remember being too bothered or embarrassed by it. Mostly I was curious. I recall asking my parents why Filipinos parents didn't let their kids do sleepovers and their response was something like, "If there's a fire in the middle of the night, who will their parents save first?"

Years later I concluded what I believed was the real reason. Sleepovers were a foreign concept in the Philippines. It wasn't like Canada or the US where the only people living in the house were parents and siblings. In most Philippine households, there were plenty of people with access to the home. Between maids, drivers, houseboys, and sometimes relatives of the maids, drivers and houseboys, it was hard to keep track of how many people were on the property at any given time. As a result, it was not common practice to let children stay overnight at any house outside their own.

Father of the Year (2005)

Now in the US, particularly when you know the parents and the family, do I think pajama parties are harmless? Sure. That said, I did observe a "slippery slope" when kids turned the corner from child to teen. "I'm sleeping over at so-and-so's house" pretty much became a license for my friends to do whatever they pleased that night. Most of their parents took the plan at face value and there was no "Let me just speak to so-and-so's parents to make sure it's OK." From the stories I heard, "spending the night" quickly turned from girls' slumber party to co-ed all-night activities.

Will Carlos and Isabel be allowed to do sleepovers? Probably, but there will be conditions. I'll definitely be speaking to the parents beforehand, and spending the night won't be a regular practice but something saved for occasions like birthday parties. Oh, and a proper invitation or evite may also be required.

I made some great friends during my short six months in Miami. Jackie and Olga here with my dad when he helped me pack up for the next move (2005)

Henny and I at Waterside when she started traveling to New York for work. Alex would tease that we were still trying to dress alike! (2007)

Natasha and I behind the booth at the PNE (1991)

With Justin and Walid (1991)

My Dad thrilled to meet Wowowee host Willie Revillame.
Can you picture this guy playing bad cop? (2006)

BBQ by the beach at English Bay in Vancouver. With family
and childhood friends Walid, Henny, Faisal and Amy (2009)

GRADUAL RELEASE

We all know stories of parents who were so strict with their children that when they finally left home they went crazy. Like, *Girls Gone Wild*[60] crazy. My mom and dad were not this type of "strict." They seemed to know exactly when and how to give us more rope. It was a gradual process and something we didn't notice until one day I realized, hey, since when am I allowed to be out this late?

When I asked my parents about it years later they explained that it was all about balance (I told you, this theme was pervasive in my upbringing). My mother would often recite what sounded like a poem, "Love will die if held too tightly, love will fly if held too lightly..."[61]

---

[60] Adult entertainment company known for videos that feature young college-age women exposing themselves and acting "wild."

[61] I have seen this poem attributed to both Dorothy Parker and Oscar Wilde. The rest of it goes, "Lightly, tightly, how do I know, whether I'm holding or letting love go." She would also quote this poem when reminding me not to be too controlling of boyfriends but that's another story.

The idea was that when we were young they would be the main source of input for our lives. They were not going to be influenced by what other kids' parents were doing (I always thought it was funny when my classmates' mom would say something like, "Let me talk to your parents. I'm sure I can convince them to let you stay the night"). They would be as strict as they felt necessary, often stepping in when we wanted to dress a certain way or do certain things. However, they were very much aware of a timeline and they adjusted ever so slightly with each stage. In our pre-teen and early teen years, my parents knew how fast some kids were growing up (especially in New York City), and they held a relatively tight grip. As we approached our late teens they saw us as more mature, they were more confident in our foundation and we felt some slack in our rope. My parents were also cognizant that it was just a matter of one or two years before we would be away from home in college. The goal was that by this time they would have given us almost as much freedom as we would experience on our own.

Talent portion of the evening (1984)

TALENT PORTION OF THE EVENING

Like most Asian kids, my brother and I took up piano and violin. Unlike Tiger Mom, however, my mother had little interest in music competitions or rankings. When my piano teacher, Mrs. Alfonso, suggested that we prepare for an upcoming regional contest my mother thanked her for thinking of us but quickly explained that she and my father weren't into the idea. They liked the discipline that went along with taking up a musical instrument (practicing regularly, improving steadily, not quitting something when it gets hard) but mostly I think they just liked the idea of us being able to play a nice tune as our contribution to a good evening.

My husband finds it hard to believe how agreeable Filipino kids are when it comes to performing upon request after big family dinners during what he calls "the talent portion of the evening." It was second nature to me and my brother (and most of our family friends) to be asked to play piano and violin whenever we had guests. There was never any protest and it just came to be expected. In retrospect it was only 10–15 minutes altogether so not a big deal when you think of the amount of appreciation from guests and pride from parents you get out of it. That said, many of our non-Filipino guests would often comment, "I could never get my children to do that."

By the time I met my husband the next generation of kids were being asked to perform at our family dinners. Most of these would take place at the Jongco residence in South Orange, New Jersey. Tito Benny and Tita Nanette Jongco were one of my parents' first friends when we moved to New York. They were both doctors (this doctor breed of Filipino immigrants was much more common on the East Coast, I was learning) and while they had their fair share of hardship immigrating to the US, by the time we met them they were comfortably successful and their big family home was perfect for entertaining. We spent most of our Easter, Thanksgiving, Christmas and New Year's celebrations there. When we first moved to New York, these were not fun holidays for me and Justin. The Jongco kids had their own set of Filipino childhood friends (akin to our JAM 4 HELP crew in Vancouver), and we were the outsiders. Justin and I entertained ourselves in their fancy bathroom (we were absolutely fascinated by the freestanding wrought iron toilet paper stand) and gigantic basement (a treasure trove of great toys we never had as kids). This changed, of course, as we got older and more social. By the time Kristen Jongco joined me at Yale the two of us had become the closest of friends and holidays at the Jongcos had turned into the best celebrations ever.

Food was as abundant as entertainment, which was provided by kids between the ages of 18 months and 18 years. Performances included everything from modern dance to concert piano to various singing renditions of *Miss Saigon* (the soundtrack of this Broadway musical became a staple in every Filipino home, thanks to Filipina singer and actress Lea Salonga). I still love seeing all of our family friends' children oblige with a smile, and I believe these performances are good for the following reasons:

1. Kids learn early on that sometimes you have to do things you don't want to.

2. It's a small token of gratitude to parents for everything they do. Most children don't realize that it isn't fun for Mom and Dad to drive around town from one activity to another not to mention the financial sacrifice involved. In many cases it only crosses their mind years later when they appreciate how well rounded they look on their college applications.

3. Getting used to being in front of a crowd is good experience no matter what you're doing.

Practicing piano (1984)

Carlos at two years old already learning about the talent portion of the evening (2012)

Justin playing violin (1983)

Our family friend Sabrina performing her routine after dinner (2012)

Singing songs from Miss Saigon (2007)

Henny and I doing a wind and string duet (1990)

The Sequence board game that typically follows the talent portion of the evening (2011)

Another karaoke night at Waterside. Security actually knocked on our door because there complaints about the noise we were making, which was particularly funny because they happened to come up while Father Diaz was singing "La Bamba" (2005)

REGULATING CHRISTMAS

*M*y *husband and I grew up in different worlds,*
but our childhood Christmas stories are very similar. Food, family
and gifts under the tree. But the gifts we both remember from back
then were more like small tokens. Thoughts that counted. We
often try to top each other with "Guess what would be wrapped
under the tree at our house?"

"Shampoo!" was one of my husband's best answers. It
wasn't until a recent birthday, however, that my husband conceded
I probably won. My father had re-gifted me with an old white
denim jacket that I wore back in high school cleaned and bleached
for the occasion.

We've celebrated Christmas together seven times now,
and each year we find ourselves exchanging disconcerted glances
as we watch the opening of presents. Let's just say that when un-
regulated this holiday doesn't bring out the best in kids. Before
one present is fully unwrapped they've moved on to the next gift.
They quickly toss the box aside when it's not on their Top 10 list
and forget about reading cards or even To and From tags. When

did Santa start accepting laundry lists of toys for each boy and girl? Probably around the same time Wal-Mart and all the other discount warehouse stores began exploding on the scene but that's beside the point.

A few years back, I remember feeling astonished after reading my cousin Natasha's blog about Christmas. She shared a sweet letter that her daughter Mariella wrote to Santa asking for a new night gown and slippers because she had been a good girl. It was so beautiful and pure and sure, a little *It's a Wonderful Life*[62] but I was amazed. It reminded me of the kids I met in Cuba during one of our family trips. Justin and I couldn't get over how excited the children were about everything. Giving them a pencil was like giving them an iPad. But Mariella didn't live in Cuba. Natasha's husband, Daniel, is a professor, they travel all over the world, and their kids have access to a ton of things. How did she keep Mariella's Santa expectations so reasonable and manage to maintain a grounded Christmas? I asked Natasha about it the next time I saw her in person and came to learn that holiday time at their home sounded very similar to the old days I remember.

Below are a few reminders I'm keeping in my mind for Carlos and Isabel:

1. Wal-Mart or no Wal-Mart, Santa just needs to bring one gift for every child. Grandparents, aunts and uncles always end up giving presents as well so no need to go overboard.

2. Kind of like eating, you should take your time opening each gift. Enjoy the process of untying the ribbon, unwrapping the paper and, most importantly, reading the card or gift tag.

---

[62] Classic American Christmas movie from the 1940s.

3. Write thank you notes. This practice makes you think about the giver more than (or as much as) the gift. Even young children can scribble or draw a picture as a thank you note.

4. Give to charity. As kids we didn't have to worry about having too many gifts or too many toys but my mother had a hunch that my children would have this experience. Even when I was still a teenager she would say things like, "You know, Jacqueline Kennedy would have John John and Caroline choose one gift and the rest they would give to charity. Isn't that a nice idea? That could be something you do with your kids since they'll grow up with so much." That was my mother, always planting seeds and reminders.

7 *had a few relationship "deal breakers"* that could be considered out of the ordinary. One of them was a negative attitude toward parents living with us. Don't get me wrong, I don't expect that living with parents or in-laws would be the first preference of any party involved, but I knew it could eventually happen so my future life partner had to be on board with the possibility. Both my mother's parents and father's parents lived with us at different times. At other points they stayed with my parents' siblings. It was the same for most of our Filipino family friends in Vancouver. In fact, I grew up thinking that most family homes include one room for the grandparents.

Once we moved to New York I quickly realized this is not the norm with most American families. It didn't necessarily mean that their families aren't close (though in some cases it did); it's just not the typical model. As such, the non-immigrants I encountered would more often than not react negatively to the very thought of their parents one day living with them, much less their in-laws.

This was not the case with Alex. He's not the type to say

things just to make himself look good so I knew he was being sincere when, even before we started dating, he would talk about taking care of his mother and expecting to take care of his future parents-in-law in the same way. When we met in Sao Paulo, Alex's father had passed away just three months earlier. A few days after meeting him at the office I met his mother who, as it turned out, was staying with him for a month (I remember thinking it was very unusual for a 29-year-old guy living in Brazil for six months to invite his mother to stay with him for such a big chunk of that time). That's when I learned about his father's passing and realized that he had arranged for his mother to spend time with him in South America as a way to stay busy during the difficult time. Many months later when we did begin dating, the idea that our future home would be open to both our parents was continuously reinforced by Alex, and I loved him for it (among other things).

The hospitality to parents and in-laws was typically extended to other family members as well. When my parents were starting out in Vancouver they lived in one-half of a duplex house. The other side was occupied by close friends, the Rebodos family. Bobot and Hetty Rebodos had three daughters, the youngest of whom, Henny, was exactly my age. Tita Hetty and my mother were on the family way[63] at the same time so a lot of their days were spent together and Henny and I became inseparable at an early age. One of my first childhood memories is being surrounded by relatives from the Philippines staying with us in the two-and-a-half bedroom duplex. There was my Lolo Seny and Lola Ely, two sets of aunts and uncles (Tito Armand and Tita Baby, Tita Lynn and Tito Rene), the parents of Tita Baby (so another set of grandparents) and a small army of cousins (Armyn, Michelle, Arvi, Joey, Jon Jon and Jay Jay). It sounds chaotic but my mother's organizational skills are second to none and somehow she managed to put a system in place that made the whole setup feel orderly and even fun. There were schedules that detailed eating and chore shifts as

---

[63] "On the family way" is my mother's way of saying "pregnant."

well as activities for each generation (outdoor mahjong for the grandparents, trips to the park for the kids) so it never got too cramped. Plus the Rebodos' doors were always open.

Staying with family worked both ways. When we first moved to New York, we stayed with relatives for months until we could settle into our own apartment. Tita Baby, Michelle and Arvi were living in a comfortable three-bedroom apartment on the Upper East Side (Tito Armand was back in the Philippines and Armyn was away at college). We were invited to stay with them while my parents sorted out our living arrangements. My father had to stay in Vancouver to tie up loose ends so my mother, Justin and I went ahead to New York since the school year was about to begin. We moved in temporarily with Tita Baby and family. I shared a room with Michelle, Justin shared with Arvi and my mother moved into the master bedroom with Tita Baby. I didn't put much thought into it at the time but looking back there's no question we invaded our cousins' space for a couple of months. Michelle was a 17-year-old high school senior, and she graciously shared with me not just her bed but also her closet. In return, she got an annoying 12-year-old cousin who would rat on her every time she got a little cozy with her boyfriend (it could be something as innocent as a hug on the couch while we were all watching a movie). Michelle never gave me any grief for it and continued to show me nothing but hospitality (thank goodness for really nice cousins from the Philippines). Arvi never complained either and made us feel right at home despite the fact that he was a 13-year-old boy who suddenly had to share his room (and all his Nintendo games) with eight-year-old Justin.

Staying with family doesn't happen as much anymore among our relatives. My cousin Natasha recently wrote me saying that she and her family would be in Singapore for a few days. When I mentioned it to Alex the first thing he said was, "Nice. Are they staying with us?" I responded, "Probably not, but I'll extend the invitation." It didn't even occur to me that Natasha and family would stay at our apartment but there would have been no question about it when I was growing up. As expected, Natasha wrote back saying she was grateful for our offer but with our new baby and all they didn't want to get in our way and would just stay at a hotel.

I know it's simply a reflection of everyone doing well and having the means to take care of their own accommodations, this way not inconveniencing anyone else. As someone who has on countless occasions both given up her room and been the reason for others to give up their rooms, I can certainly appreciate this sentiment. Still, part of me can't help but feel like we lose something as we get more comfortable. Surely spending many evenings together helps break down barriers more than having a dinner or two. Some of my best childhood memories came from staying with family. After the awkward first day making forced small talk, by night two you're exchanging family jokes (and sometimes secrets).

As inconvenient and uncomfortable as it could be at times, staying with family gave us some invaluable skills:

1. Adaptability. Maybe you'll sleep on the floor and your cousin can take the bed, maybe all the kids will camp out on sleeping bags in the living room. Whatever the setup you learn to go with it.

2. Social competence. It's not always easy breaking the ice with relatives you haven't met before or people from another country with whom you have little in common, but that's an invaluable skill to carry with you the rest of your life.

3. Hosting flair. They don't call it inconvenience for no reason. There are basic things you need to do as a host family: from getting up earlier than you'd like to putting breakfast on the table to offering to take relatives out on the town when you'd rather be getting downtime on the couch. These will serve you well in the future with in-laws and other guests.

Mom and Alex before we watched *The Color Purple on Broadway* (2006)

Cheesy family photo by the Citibank ATMs in Chinatown (2007)

CLOSE IS AN UNDERSTATEMENT

One of the things my husband quickly noticed about my family was how close we are. He met them for the first time when we were both doing expat assignments in Sao Paulo. We weren't dating then and, in fact, for the short period that we did know each other we butted heads on more than one occasion. We were introduced right outside the Citi offices on Avenida Paulista on my first day at work. I was with my fellow management associate Shuana, and Alex was with his peer Theo. Alex and Theo had been in Brazil for a month before we arrived so they would be able to show us the ropes. We were all housed at the same Marriott Executive Apartments so we naturally started to spend time together, whether driving to work, taking Portuguese classes or exploring the city. I was initially very attracted to Alex. He fit the description of tall, dark and handsome; he was smart; and he was funny. After the first week or so, however, it started to become clear that we were going to have a love-hate relationship. As we got more comfortable around each other, Alex started poking at me more frequently. At first I took it as playful teasing, maybe even flirtation, but it soon got to a point that it was too often for my threshold. It felt as though he scoffed at everything I said.

We would be out at dinner with a group of colleagues having a conversation about life and where we wanted to take our careers. I would be saying something like, "Eventually I may want to move from private to public sector. I just want to feel like I'm making a contribution to society."

Alex would laugh. "Who speaks like that?"

"What do you mean who speaks like that? I speak like that."

"Right, I'm sure you're having trouble sleeping at night because you're not 'contributing to society.'"

How dare he mock me! That's it. He was off my "potentials" list.

These exchanges continued for months until my family came to visit me for Christmas. My father and Justin arrived first since my mother needed to finish up the school semester. They met Alex and Shauna at breakfast the morning after they arrived, and the five of us made plans for dinner. That evening my father and Justin came to pick me up from the office. Shauna and I were sharing a car, and she offered to let my family use it while they were visiting. Just like in Miami, my father was going to teach me how to drive in Sao Paulo, this time using stick shift. I was practicing on the roads around our neighborhood when Alex and Shauna drove by and saw me learning how to shift gears.

"That was really cute how your dad was teaching you to drive," Alex commented on our way to the restaurant. It felt like one of the first non-sarcastic things he had said to me in weeks. Everyone had a nice time at dinner, and we all made plans to the do the same the following day. I started noticing that the more time Alex spent with my family, the nicer he seemed toward me. When my mother arrived a week later the two of us had become quite friendly. He wasn't rolling his eyes or mocking me and he seemed to take a genuine interest in the stories my parents and Justin were telling about our family.

I came to learn that it took a while to build trust with Alex. Chalk it up to eight years in the army or a string of negative experiences with certain people but whatever the case he had become a little cynical to say the least. He admitted to thinking I was "disingenuous" when we first met. He figured I was putting on an act ("How could she really be this bubbly?" he later confessed to thinking) so he didn't take anything I said at face value. "Then I met her family and realized, 'They're all like this!'" I have overheard him explain to others.

Alex continued to find out just how close we are in my family. He always says that before he met us he never considered raising children in New York City. He thought of Manhattan as a great place to work and socialize but not the place you would have kids. He said he completely changed his

Our first date. We saw Phantom of the Opera in Portuguese (2006)

mind after spending time with my family. When Alex and I began seriously dating upon my return to New York, we spent every day together. We worked in the same building midtown, and two to three times a week we would take a taxi straight from the office to my parents' place at Waterside Plaza where Justin would also be meeting us for dinner. For many people this arrangement could be a little excessive but Alex didn't appear to mind. In fact, it seemed like he enjoyed the experience of regular family meals in Manhattan. To him it was reminiscent of life in a small town. Two years later my parents gave up the Waterside residence and moved into an apartment they had purchased in newly gentrifying Harlem. By this time Alex and I were married and we followed suit since our midtown studio was getting too cramped. We ended up living down the block from my parents on 116th Street and Fifth

Avenue, and the family dinners became even more frequent until we moved to Singapore.

In addition to weekday dinners, Sundays had always been designated family days (even when Justin and I were both out of the house and in our 20s). They typically started with my parents picking us up at my midtown studio. We'd hop in the Mitsubishi Montero (same one they use today) and then proceed down Second Avenue to Epiphany Church. Once Mass was done, we would get back in the car and drive to New Jersey. I don't know if deep down we missed the suburbs, but hitting the Jersey malls was a family pastime. We had our favorite, of course. When Jersey Gardens opened its doors in 1999 it quickly became our go-to Sunday destination. It was just off the Turnpike, had 200+ outlet stores, a great food court and an AMC Loews theater. What more could you ask for? We would park by the movie theater since there were always spots (it worked out for us since we knew that's where we would end up) and then check out what was playing. It didn't have to be particularly good. Mostly the movies served the purpose of killing time between meals. Don't get me wrong, it was always great when we could catch *A Beautiful Mind* or another Oscar-nominated movie, but our plans wouldn't change if the only things playing were *Mall Cop* and *Water Boy*.[64]

From there we would head straight to the food court where we typically shared two Cajun Grill combos and a slice or two from Sbarros. After lunch we'd split up and agree on a designated time (usually an hour later) to meet back at the food court by Cinnabon. My mother and I would start off together usually at Benetton and then make our way to Last Call by Neiman Marcus, both of which were slam dunks for deals. Dresses originally marked as $299 had become $119, minus 50%. And wait, did it have a green sticker? Minus an additional 30%. Normally by the time I finished paying for my bargain basement priced blouse my mother

---

[64] *A Beautiful Mind* is the Oscar-nominated drama starring Russell Crowe. *Mall Cop* and *Water Boy* are both slapstick comedies starring actor-comedians Kevin James and Adam Sandler, respectively.

would still be browsing through the green sticker rack. We'd part ways so I could still get in time for BCBG and Club Monaco on my own.

The meeting time always came around fast and typically my father would be the first in front of Cinnabon. He'd have a Haggar bag in tow and Justin would come around the corner and tease, "How many khaki pants do you need?" My father would take out three pairs of pants, "Guess how much?" This was always part of the fun. One would be for him, and the other two were for the *balikbayan* box. Justin didn't have a go-to store per se but more often than not if he had a bag it was a button down or polo from Banana Republic. "How much?" it was my father's turn to ask. No matter what price you said you'd get the same gasp-filled reaction. "*What? That much?* You should come with me, I can get you a shirt like that for $5." My mother would arrive last but she'd have multiple items and as she pulled out each piece it would sound like Neiman Marcus was giving away clothes. "And this one could be for Lola Adoring," she would be referring to my father's mother. That was always a surefire way to make him happy.

After show and tell we would sit down to split a Cinnabon if there was time before the movie, otherwise we would walk across the parking lot to AMC Loews with a quick stop at the car to drop off our purchases. If we didn't have time for Cinnabon one of us would get in line for a popcorn/soda combo that we would all share. This snack would tide us over until after the movie. We would have dinner on the way back to Manhattan alternating between Vietnamese and Filipino restaurants located by the Holland Tunnel. After dinner my father would make a play for one last stop, the international grocery. By this point the mere mention would make the rest of us groan because it was already getting dark and the Sunday night blues were beginning to set in. "At least we have to stop for gas." New Jersey gas was the cheapest in the nation, and no way would my father miss out on such a deal.

All this time together definitely made us close. Justin and I amuse ourselves recalling how compelled we felt to tell our parents *everything*. If you were one of our peers and thought you could count on us to keep a secret from the grownups you'd better think again. Our cousins learned the hard way. One summer when we were visiting Tita Elma's family in San Pablo our older cousins were assigned to watch us for the day. It happened to be a Sunday, but the group consensus was to skip church. "We'll just enjoy the beach today. Just don't tell Tita Nore and Tito Didi," they would joke. Poor guys, they had no idea with whom they were dealing. Justin and I tried not to tell our parents but the guilt consumed us. We had never before kept anything from our parents and not once in our memory missed church. On the drive back to Manila I started noticing Justin's head turning side to side as he tried to look out the window in several directions. He was quietly mouthing things, "No left turn... Jollibee Next Exit... Manila 50 miles..."

"What are you doing?" I asked.

"Since we missed church I promised God I would read everything I saw out loud," Justin answered. Talk about Catholic guilt at its worst. I told my parents about Justin's self- imposed penance. They talked to him and explained he didn't do anything wrong but, boy, my cousins never heard the end of it.

Family fun in the streets of Sao Paulo (2005)

As the years went by we continued our practice of family confessions. When Justin called from college one night he was describing how everyone in his dorm was smoking marijuana. "I think I might want to try it too," he told us on a conference call. "Wait, Justin,"my mother quipped, "Wait until you're home for Thanksgiving so we can all try it together. It's better you're with us instead of with strangers." As usual, the woman had a point. We never ended up getting high together as a family but the fact that Justin and I were always comfortable being so open with our parents is something I'll never forget.

Mom and I in Las Vegas at The Beatles LOVE by Cirqué du Soleil (2007)

Justin being sworn in after passing the New Jersey State Bar (2006)

After Justin's swearing in ceremony my family went a little crazy with the camera again (2006)

Just after getting engaged (2008)

Enjoying a New York City pedicab ride (2009)

Pacquiao-Hatton fight in Las Vegas (2009)

Cheering on Manny Pacquaio from home (2010)

Birthday dinner at Waterside (2009)

Climbing the Bandeiras Monument just outside Ibirapu-
era Park in Sao Paulo (2006)

Citibank Christmas party in Sao
Paulo (2005)

View from our Rio hotel
room (2006)

With some of our
expat circle in Sao
Paulo (2006)

Mom and Lloyd Blankfein, CEO of Goldman Sachs (2008)

Mom and Mayor Michael Bloomberg at the inauguration of the Kalahari
Harlem condo, where we lived for two years (2008)

Receiving the President's
Volunteer Service Award
(2004)

At the Nobel
Institute in Oslo
representing the
Business Council
for Peace (2004)

PURSUING DREAMS, LIVING REALITY

I've been working full-time since college and while I've enjoyed building a career in marketing and financial services, there are also other things I'd like to pursue. I can't help but feel a little wistful when I see some of my non full-time working girlfriends throwing themselves into projects they love whether it's starting their own jewelry line, climbing Mount Everest or writing a book.[65] I feel a twinge sorry for myself as I think that I may not be able to do many of those things until I stop working. Then I remember my mother's example of doing it anyway. She had a full-time job straight from college all the way to the age of retirement but somehow she managed to pursue her passions. When I say things like, "Once I stop working I can finally focus on the book I've wanted to write," she responds with, "No need to wait. Just manage your time and you can do it while working. It will be even more rewarding."

This perspective is similar to the advice she and my father would

---

[65] When I met my friend Christine Amour-Levar shortly after moving to Singapore she was doing two out of three! Her book is called *The Smart Girl's Handbook to Being Mummylicious*.

give me when I first started working. Like many others, I went the practical route. I had student loans and other bills to pay so I took a job in the private sector (aka "selling out" if you were a fresh grad from Yale). Meanwhile some of my friends (mostly those who came out of college debt-free) were taking on "save the world" projects over which we spent many a late night pontificating in the dorm rooms. With a little envy and loads of admiration I watched one of my best friends Kristen lead an NGO called FACES[66] that was lobbying to clean up former US military bases in the Philippines. Somehow selling credit cards didn't feel as meaningful and I'd think to myself, "I guess it won't be until after student loans are

paid when I can work on something that I would be that passionate about..." Again, my parents would remind me that there was no reason to wait. I then started pushing myself to identify opportunities to help the community in my own way using the resources and platforms that I had.

Habitat for Humanity's Jimmy Carter Work Project in Puebla, Mexico (2004)

When I heard that Citi was launching an online remittance product I saw a chance to put the Filipino community on the company's radar. I had come across one of the marketing decks for the new product and quickly observed that there were plans to promote it to all the top remittance-receiving countries except the Philippines. There were pages focused on how to target the Mexican, Indian, Chinese, Latin American and Caribbean communities but nowhere could I find a mention of the Philippines, which I thought was strange considering they were the second largest remittance market for the US directly behind Mexico.

I reached out to contacts within the bank to find out why

---

[66] Filipino-American Coalition for Environmental Solutions.

this was the case. As it turned out the product managers had been trying for several months to figure out how to reach the Filipino community (they had seen the data too) but they were coming up short even after multiple meetings with various ethnic marketing agencies. What they quickly learned was that Filipinos in the United States were not very easy to reach or target. They were the second largest Asian population in the US after the Chinese but this fact surprised many because generally speaking Filipino-Americans received relatively little recognition as a demographic group despite their sheer number. The American occupation of the Philippines had established English as one of the official languages of the country (along with Filipino and Spanish) so most Filipinos came to the US assimilating relatively quickly into American society taking up jobs in offices, hospitals and other mainstream lines of work. Whenever people ask me why there aren't many Filipino restaurants or why they've never seen a Filipino-town (equivalent to Chinatown or Korea-town) I provide the explanation above. As a result of this easy assimilation Filipino-Americans are sometimes referred to as "the invisible minority."

My friends have always commented about how elated I get when I find out that someone has Filipino ancestry. Something inside me just wants to shout it out to the world. For as long as I remember I have always felt this way. Maybe I was just astute and detected the whole "invisible minority" phenomenon or maybe it's just in my blood.

My parents often tell the story about the time I came to the hospital right after Justin was born. I was four years old and beaming with pride as I peered through the glass window of the nursery admiring my new baby brother. A Caucasian couple walked over and stood next to us. "So sweet," the woman told her husband as she pointed to Justin, "Look at that cute Chinese baby!"

"He's not Chinese," I informed them. "He's Filipino." They were a little taken by surprise as were my parents. The woman kindly apologized and I responded with a smile. It was OK but I just wanted her to know.

Since then I've been educating everyone around me about anyone who has Filipino lineage.

Here's my list of famous people who are Filipino/partly Filipino:

The obvious ones who always proudly represent the Philippines:

- Manny Pacquiao
- Lea Salonga
- Charice
- Jessica Sanchez
- Arnel Pineda

The not-so-obvious ones who go out of their way to let people know they have Filipino ancestry (they do more interviews than they need to with the Philippine press, they incorporate Filipino associations into their jokes or their songs, they help advocate Filipino causes, e.g., Filipino veteran rights, etc.):

- Rob Schneider
- Lou Diamond Phillips
- Black Eyed Peas Apl.D.Ap
- Darren Criss
- Bruno Mars

The ones who may already mention their Filipino heritage though I wish they would do it more often:

- Enrique Iglesias
- Cheryl Burke
- Nicole Scherzinger
- Vanessa Hudgens
- Vanessa Manillo
- Mark-Paul Gosselaar
- Tia Carrere

- Phoebe Cates
- The artist formerly known as Prince

The ones who are off my radar (only because I'm not as up-to-date as I used to be on all the latest celebrities) but on everyone else's—they come up in articles like "Stars you didn't know had Filipino blood" so they must be included here:

- Rachel Grant (James Bond)
- Mark Dacascos (Iron Chef)
- Anna Marie Perez de Tagle (Hannah Montana)
- Jasmine Villegas (Justin Bieber's tour)
- Hailee Steinfeld (True Grit)
- Batista (Wrestler)
- Kirk Hammett (Metallica)
- Mutya Buena (British group Sugababes)

I also find myself bragging about famous Filipinos outside of showbiz:

- Loida Nicolas Lewis (businesswoman and philanthropist)
- Monique Lhuillier (fashion designer)
- Josie Natori (fashion designer)
- Erik Spoelstra (Miami Heat coach)
- Tim Lincecum (San Francisco Giants pitcher)
- Diosdado Banatao (successful tech entrepreneur in Silicon Valley)
- Rico Hizon (news anchor on BBC World News)

To my delight, the list of Filipinos in the spotlight has been growing increasingly, especially in the last several years. Reality TV talent competitions are providing Filipinos with a platform to gain more recognition in singing, dancing and cooking. (And let's not even get started on Manny Pacquaio and how much he has done to put the Philippines even more prominently on the map.)

It's a great sign when my husband says, "I can't believe how excited you still get every time you hear that someone's Filipino. Filipinos are everywhere."

It certainly didn't feel this way a decade ago when Citi was trying to figure out how to market to Filipino-Americans. The business heads were thrilled when I offered to introduce them to my contacts at the Philippine Consulate and other leaders in the community. Citi ended up becoming a major sponsor for our series of nationwide events commemorating Independence Day. The bank got exposure to a market they had been trying to reach and the Filipino community found a corporate sponsor they had wanted to secure. What more, I was able to work on something I was passionate about while doing my day job.

Most graduation keynote addresses have a common message: Do what you love and follow your passion. As inspiring as they are, I can't help but think my mother could have a counter speech that might just better serve the majority of those graduating. It would go something like this: Try to find a job where you do what you love but if it doesn't happen right away and you have bills to pay, find a job where you'll pick up skills and contacts that can be applied to passion projects on the side. You can pursue these at the same time and, who knows, one of them may ultimately lead to your dream job.

It may not be a sexy speech and you probably won't find inspiring excerpts from it reposted on Facebook but its message might put many fresh grads in a better place years down the line. Many people follow their bliss only to find misery. They pass up plenty of opportunities to do only what they love but 10, 20 years later they are left with overwhelming debt and overall unhappiness. Don't get me wrong, I derive inspiration from Steve Jobs speeches just as much as the next person (maybe even more) but taking the typical graduation address literally will only work for a small percentage of the population. After all, how many Steve Jobs, Bill Gates, Mark Zuckerbergs or Matt Damons and Ben Afflecks can there be? It's like the other day when I was watching *X Factor.*[67] One of the contestants didn't make it through the first round and said, "That's okay. Like they say, you have to just keep following your dreams, right?" Simon Cowell responded, "Only for the small number of people who are really lucky and really good."

Of course, the situation varies by circumstances. If you are fortunate to have some flexibility and financial means, or your raw talent supersedes everything else, then following your bliss may be the best advice for you. For the majority of people out there, however, it probably wouldn't be such a bad idea to take a job with upside career potential that in some way aligns with their interests (even if not directly with their dreams). It doesn't mean there is no place for passion. My mother worked as a teacher for years but continued to work on side projects where she could apply as well as further develop her talent. Once my brother and I were out of the house and done with school, she had even more room to pursue her art. It was never too late and her work before then actually ended up helping her as an artist. Since she taught at the United Nations International School for 18 years, influential people from the international community were attracted to her art. They have admired her work so much that many of them have invited her back to their home countries to exhibit.

Speaking at event for Filipino Young Professionals hosted by CORE (Collaborative Opportunities for Raising Empowerment) in New York City (2006)

In my case, I'm passionate about all things global, and working at a place like Citi has allowed me to do business with

---

[67] Another TV music competition created by Simon Cowell.

colleagues and clients across over 40 countries while living in several cities around the world. I didn't necessarily grow up dreaming about working for a big bank but building a career in financial services has allowed me to facilitate various microfinance projects in emerging markets. I've also been able to use my marketing skills to help entrepreneurs in developing countries scale their businesses and create employment opportunities in different parts of the globe.

Pursuing your dreams while living your reality can be done. It does, however, require more creativity, discipline and patience to achieve. The day may come when everything has fallen into place. You land the job of your dreams. The start-up you joined goes public. You find yourself with enough financial cushion that you don't have to work anymore. In the meantime, don't take for granted all the things you can do along the way.

I don't often go around quoting profound literary excerpts (as you can tell from my citations, which are mostly TV show-related), but one in particular has always resonated with me:

> "If you prepare yourself at every point as well as you can, with whatever means you may have, however meager they may seem, you will be able to grasp opportunity for broader experience when it appears."[68]

> —Eleanor Roosevelt

---

[68] Roosevelt, Eleanor, *The Autobiography of Eleanor Roosevelt* (New York: Da Capo Press, 1961).

At the Philippine Independence Day Parade with Loida Nicolas Lewis, Filipino born American businesswoman, philanthropist, and civic leader (2002)

Celebrating Citi's 200 year anniversary in Singapore with former CEO Vikram Pandit (2012)

Sharing a laugh with Justin during the Philippine Independence Day Parade (2008)

Dinner out with good friends including Chloe Drew, Executive Director of Council of Urban Professions and Karl Williams, Yale alum and entrepreneur (2009)

Filipino pride (2008)

First official Filipinotown I've come across is in LA (2005)

$\mathcal{W}$*hile this book is not intended* to be a prescriptive guide of any sort there are a few practical tips I've picked up from my mother that I think are worth sharing. Many of them are multi-beneficial—good for the pocketbook, the waistline and overall sensible living.

Shopping at upscale department stores
- Dress up. As you walk by fabulous clothes and gorgeous displays you'll feel better about yourself if you're looking your best (you may even feel less compelled to buy everything if you already look and feel great).

- Visit the concierge—one of the best kept secret at Bloomingdales, Saks, Neiman Marcus and the like. Check in your coat and bags at the door so you can comfortably enjoy browsing and taking in ideas. Get a good chance to find out if there are any current sales or specials. Some stores like Macy's Herald Square even offer visitors a "discount pass."

- Get the most value out of every purchase. According to my

mother, with each item bought you are entitled to one gift box, a generous portion of tissue paper, a crisp shopping bag and ribbon if they have it. 1 item = 1 gift box, 1 portion of tissue paper, 1 shopping bag, 1 ribbon. 2 items = 2 boxes, 2 portions of tissue paper, 2 shopping bags, 2 ribbons. 3 items... you get the idea. Don't underestimate how handy all this will come in when you're scurrying around the house one day putting a gift together a few minutes before you need to leave for a party.

- GWP. Wait until Estee Lauder, Lancome or Clinique promotes their "gift with purchase" before replacing your lipstick or foundation. You end up with a couple extra lipsticks, mascara, eye shadow, sample moisturizer and a beautiful cosmetic case.

- For the most pleasant shopping experience, take a leisurely break and enjoy quality ambience at the café. Sit down for a coffee or split the soup and sandwich combo. The atmosphere alone is usually worth it. Plus many of these places often have great bread baskets and big refreshing jugs of water.

- Upscale department stores do have affordable clothing, but they won't be the first things you see displayed. That said, these stores also have some of the biggest sales so it is best to go at an off peak time, say, during Barney's twice-annual sales.

Eating out

- Time of day factors into how much you spend at restaurants. If you want to try out a celebrity chef restaurant, go there for lunch. You'll get pretty much the same experience and a good taste of what it offers.

- Time of year is another variable. Want to use Valentine's

Day as an excuse to try out that fancy restaurant? Have an eve celebration and do it on February 13th.

- Dress up. They'll want to seat you by the window. And if they don't, ask to be seated by the window or the equivalent best seat in the house.

- Ask for extra plates and always share entrées. Good for the figure and the wallet. Formula that we use: If we're a party of 4, we order 3 main dishes. Party of 5, 3 mains. Party of 6, 4 mains. Party of 10, 6 mains. Divide the number of people and add one! As the party gets bigger you can sprinkle in a couple of appetizers.

- Dividing/slicing up. Think Jesus multiplying the fish and loaves of bread. One slice of pizza can make a dozen mini triangles. One burger cut into quarters and you get sliders for everyone to share.

- Ask for an extra chair. No need to be uncomfortable with purses and bags.

- Drinks, especially alcoholic ones, add a significant amount to the tab. Have cocktails at home and when it's just family and kids, limit beverages to ice water for everyone.

Eating in
- Establish menus for the week. You'll save money (and time) on weekly groceries when you know exactly what you're getting.

- When heating leftovers, make a circle in the middle to heat more evenly. This is a lifesaving technique with lasagna.

- Pack away some portion of leftovers in the freezer as well as the fridge. This way nothing goes bad and you always have something readily available to eat.

- Even when you're only having take-out, serve the food on real plates and use your nice silverware.

- Garnish even when you don't have guests. Everyday Filipino food is delicious, but a lot of the dishes can have an overall brown coloring. Sliced green onions, hardboiled egg, lemon and sliced shrimp can significantly enhance the meal.

Hosting

- Incorporate into your menu make-ahead dishes that reheat well. On the day of the dinner, you should only be putting stuff in the oven and doing other finishing touches so you're ready to entertain the minute the first guest arrives. It's not fun for anyone when the host has to slave away in the kitchen and miss the socializing.

- Say yes when your friends ask if they can bring something. No such thing as too many salads or desserts. Your guests will feel good about contributing something, and it's one thing less for you to do.

- Never put everything out at once. Always ration and save some of each dish to bring out in phases later.

- Always have a little entertainment. Whether it's your child playing an instrument after dinner, your guests doing what they do best, or everyone singing a song in unison —something that goes with the theme of the party, e.g., "What a wonderful world" for a baby's baptism.

- Assign your kids jobs to help clean and get your house

ready as much as you can before guests arrive (polishing silver, bathroom duty, etc. can be easily divvied up).

- Set aside a few minutes before guests arrive to have a glass of wine and put on music.

Around the house

- Save those shopping bags. They always make for good carriers of gifts, desserts, etc.

- Doilies. A thing of the '80s? Maybe, but still a fabulous touch when putting out cookies and other snacks.

- Always have tissue paper and ribbon handy. You will never fail to find a use.

- Keep stamps and envelopes ready in a desk drawer so you can send out thank you notes right away.

- Scissors. Before Bounty came out with their "Select-a-Size" product, my mother was already halving the paper towels because she thought most uses required only half the dimension. She does this with Ikea napkins, cotton pads and the like.

Travel

- When packing, throw in some extra plastic bags, i.e., grocery bags, Ziploc bags, etc. in the side pocket. You'll use them for wet clothes, shoes, jewelry, toiletries.

- Before leaving the house, move a few dishes to the freezer from the fridge. They'll go bad in the fridge and when you get back from the trip you'll be grateful to have something ready to eat. No one feels like cooking or doing grocery shopping upon returning home.

- Always have extra plastic/paper cups handy. Even the small Dixie cups that you rinse with at the dentist. In the car, on outings, etc. you'd be surprised how far one can of soda, one bottle of Gatorade or one Starbucks coffee can go when extra cups are readily available.

- Even if the kids are out of diapers, bring baby wipes. They're good for washing hands, cleaning toilet seats, and wiping down restaurant tables.

- Always have a pashmina in your bag. They can dress up your outfit or serve as another layer or blanket when the plane, train or car gets cold.

Others

- If you're feeling sick put a little makeup on and try to freshen up, wash your hair. Sloppy clothes, pale skin and greasy hair will not make you feel any better.

- When shopping at the food market without a car (a la city life), don't use a cart; use a basket so you know how much you can carry on your walk back.

- When you have a baby, always bring along a *lampin*, a thin diaper cloth. It's small enough to stuff in the side pocket of your purse and can serve as a blanket or diaper if necessary even if your baby uses disposable diapers .

There are a few other practical tips that require a little more detail.

KEEP A YELLOW LEGAL PAD
(OR DIGITAL EQUIVALENT)

*O*ne *of my mother's favorite things to do* is write down personal goals. On a regular basis she would pull out her yellow legal pad and say, "Let's do our goals."

The yellow legal pad was a fixture on my mother's desk. Going down the rows on the left side of the page she would write out the years, e.g., 1990, 1991, 1992, 1993, 1994... Going across the page from right to the left she would create columns, e.g., UNIS, Art, Community. She would then draft ideas for things she wanted to achieve. For example, in 1993 she would aim to be part of a group art exhibit at Gallery X in New York. Two years later, 1995, she would target a solo art exhibit at the Metropolitan Museum of Art in the Philippines, etc. This would all set her up nicely to apply for the Pollack Krasner grant in 1998...

Typically goals would be sketched five years out, though in my mother's case she would jot down ideas as far as 10 years down the line. We would sit down together and I'd draft my own in the same format. I'm convinced it's the only way I got to experience living and working in different continents, all the while doing an executive MBA program based out of New York. Putting these ideas in writing provides clear direction in your day-to-day life and always makes you feel like you're working toward something meaningful.

(Right page) Lenore RS Lim: *Blossoms 4*, Lithography, chine colle, 44" x 30", 2010

Blossoms 4

Lorne H. Zinn 2011

The very process of writing this book reflects one of the most important reminders from my mother: Don't underestimate how much you can do when you make the best use of your time.

Once you have drafted your strategic goals, you need a tactical schedule to manage day-to-day activities that align with your objectives. I knew I had a limited window to put this book together. I would be on maternity leave for four months, but during this time I would also be at home with a two-year-old son and a newborn daughter. Thankfully we have a great helper so the work around the house is in good hands. In consultation with my mother I developed a schedule for Carlos, Isabel and myself that carved out time for writing,—mostly during Carlos' nap and Isa's feedings (My Brest Friend[69] is a lifesaver). I determined how much I needed to get done by the end of Mont h 1, Month 2, Month 3 and Month 4 and then figured out how much time each day I had to set aside for writing.

---

[69] My #1 recommendation for nursing pillow. Isa would be on my lap sleeping for a good couple of hours after feeding and I could write in peace.

My *mother is always prepared.* Trapped in traffic for half an hour, she's got a snack pack in her tote. Stuck in a waiting room during lunchtime, she's got a candy bar in her purse. Grabbing coffee at an independent café that only uses raw sugar, she's got Equal on reserve for Alex—who only uses sweetener—in her pocketbook. Beyond handy items, my mother is always prepared for meetings, talks and life in general. I remember watching her sit down one day to write introductory remarks for an art exhibit she had organized to promote emerging artists from the Philippines. I thought to myself, *She doesn't need to do that. She knows the artists like the back of her hand.* I used to believe that if I knew a topic well I could just speak about it off the top of my head. It's more natural that way, right? Wrong. I've since learned that the make-it-up-as-you-go-along approach may get you by most of the time but there will inevitably come a day when you want to bang your head over not taking the time to be prepared. Whether it's your best friend's wedding or a big business meeting, you'll know that you blew it.

When I was in the second grade, my teacher Sister Jean assigned me to do the First Reading at the school-wide Mass. Every week three children would be picked to read at church (First

Reading, Responsorial Psalm, and Second Reading). Since it was a regular occurrence at St. Michael's I didn't think it was too much of a big deal. My mother, however, thought the contrary. In her mind, this privilege merited substantial preparation. First, she had me type out the reading on a cue card so I could become completely familiar with the passage. Plus, she didn't want me walking up to the big intimidating Bible on the lectern and fumbling with the pages trying to find my spot. Once I learned all the biblical terms in the text she wanted me to practice reciting it in my "speaking voice" ("The sound needs to carry across the big church"). This required me to practically memorize the reading since I had to look up most of the time ("Your voice will be directed to the floor if you keep looking down at the words"). I didn't think all the rehearsal was necessary but when the following week came and it was my turn to go up to do the reading I had to admit that I felt pretty good about it. My mother didn't even have to say I told you so. The following day Sister Jean announced that Father Newman wanted to publicly recognize me for the great job. He appreciated that I took the assignment seriously and wanted to reinforce this practice with the other kids. He also gave me a prayer book, a special candle and a box of Smarties.

I wish I had remembered this experience 20-odd years later when I was scheduled to speak at a regional business conference in Barcelona. I was working for a senior executive named Vicky Bindra at the time. Vicky was sharp, witty and, boy, could he deliver a presentation. A former Bain consultant, he knew exactly how to tell a good story, engage the audience and propose a compelling solution. It was definitely in my best interest to impress him so I must have logged in over a hundred hours working on the content for my section. I was planning to do a little dress rehearsal in the hotel room the night before my presentation but by the time I got back from dinner with colleagues it was late and I figured I'd have time in the morning. When the sun came up, however, I realized that between getting showered, dressed and meeting colleagues for breakfast, I actually didn't have much time to prepare after all. *It should be fine though. I know this information down pat.*

When it came time for my topic, I went to the front of the room and began to speak. To my dismay, I found myself rambling a little through the pages. Sure, I knew the content well but I didn't have a game plan for how I wanted to talk through. What more, I found myself turning my back to the audience quite often to look at the slides on the projector screen (where was my mother to remind me about the importance of my voice carrying across the room?). It ended up going OK since I was still the subject matter expert but as I walked back to my seat afterwards I couldn't shake the sense of mediocrity. *Maybe I'm being too hard on myself. You are your worst critic, right?*

Wrong. My boss was pretty harsh too. Well, as harsh as I've ever experienced since I started working anyway. I had grown accustomed to high praise after leaving these kinds of meetings, which is probably why I took for granted the need to prepare for this one. *Nailed it,* I would always just know as I got to the final page. Not this time. When Vicky and I got back to New York and debriefed on the Barcelona meeting, he gave me some feedback. "On a scale of 1 to 10, I would give you a 10 for content and a 6 for delivery." *Holy, worse than I thought.* He proceeded to describe how he prepares for all his talks, big or small. He asked me how long I thought it took him to prep for the wrap-up session during our department offsite one month earlier. I had just assumed he got up and the words flowed out of him. He was always so articulate and succinct. "Two hours," he told me. *Whoa. If Vicky Bindra took two hours to prepare for his department offsite, who was I to think I could wing it at a regional conference?*

Lesson learned. A little preparation would have gone a long way. Vicky was a new boss and he had very few data points on me—I hated that this was one of them. I knew I had squandered an opportunity to make a great impression. Vicky is now President of MasterCard Asia Pacific and while the two of us are in touch regularly and he seems to thinks highly of me at this point, I still find myself wishing I could go back in time to prepare for that damn Barcelona meeting.

Before our wedding reception (2009)

TO BE CONTINUED...

There are some things my mother does that I admire but I don't think I'll ever be disciplined enough to do. On a frequent basis she takes time to demonstrate how to efficiently roll a stack of coins or tie a pretty bow around a piece of cake. She'll quickly pick up on my level of engagement and say, "You're never going to do this, are you?" She'll continue, "I guess you don't need to do this for now. But if you ever find yourself in a time of war at least you'll know how to be resourceful... ."

Things my mother does that I should but probably won't do:

- Collect coins from around the house, roll them and bring them to the bank[70]
- Slice up a fruitcake (or any cake with this density, e.g., pound cake, food for the gods, etc.), individually wrap them in foil, tissue and ribbon before going to anyone's house during the holidays

---

[70] My husband wants me to footnote for the record that he brings coins to the bank for our family.

- Sell things on the side for extra pocket money (South Sea pearls from the Philippines, macramé jewelry that she handmade, etc.)
- Extend individual packs of Swiss Miss or Nestle 3 in 1s into 2–3 servings
- Open gifts carefully, undoing one piece of scotch tape at a time so wrapping paper can be folded and reused
- Use taxis minimally

Things my mother does that I do/intend to do:

- Keep Christmas gifts limited and donate extra toys to charity
- Make water the default response when asked for beverage orders
- Not give money (even if I have spare change handy) every time my kids see a candy machine or mini ride in the shopping mall
- Not let my kids go around saying, "I'm bored"
- Match money spent on a family party with donation to School of Love and Hope or an equivalent cause
- Split entrees at a restaurant
- Ask my kids to perform after dinner

I write this book knowing that I can never exactly replicate the experiences that my husband or I had but if we keep a balanced perspective and do even a fraction of the things we say we want to, then I believe our children (and we ourselves) will be much better off for it. More than anything these stories serve as reminders of times and ways I don't want to forget. I realize we're not going to start giving up hotels altogether but at least I want to be aware of the experiences our kids may miss by not staying with family. We can probably afford every toy and gadget they ask for, but we can also control the quantity and frequency by which they receive them. You need to experience sacrifice and longing before you can fully appreciate what you have, and kids who grow up too comfortably may miss out on this lesson if a concerted effort isn't made to teach them.

Reminders from my mother include everything from raising kids to developing relationships to achieving your dreams, all of which I want to pass along to children. There are books out there like *Never Eat Alone*[71] and courses like *SMART Goal Setting*.[72] People spend hundreds of thousands of dollars on schools for the networking and relationships they foster. My mother didn't have any such formal training but somehow these things came naturally. Even more impressive is that she makes an impact without trying. She simply lives her life the best way she knows how, and it makes a difference to so many people around her. Often times she is unaware of it. On a few occasions I've experienced these kinds of "mom moments." That is, when people go out of their way to do something kind for me saying what a difference I've made yet I have to think twice about what that could have been. I feel happy when I realize what happened—like I did something right.

When I first started working at Citi in New York there was a cleaning lady who would come by everyday around 5 p.m to empty the trash. She had a very warm demeanor, and I was always happy to engage her in conversation at the end of the day. Her name was Maria, and she was from the Dominican Republic. At one point I asked if I could practice my Spanish with her, and she was delighted. It was great for me as my language skills hadn't been put into practice much since I studied abroad in college. Through our exchanges I learned she had a son and daughter in high school. I shared with her pictures of my family from our recent trip to the Philippines.

When I got promoted my boss finally managed to secure an office for me, which was not an easy task given the internal politics and lack of space. It was kind of a makeshift office with a hodgepodge of furniture including an old desk, mismatched

---

[71] Excellent book about networking written by Keith Ferrazzi.

[72] SMART is an acronym for Specific, Measurable, Attainable, Relevant and Time Bound.

chairs, a broken file cabinet and a wobbly conference table but I didn't care. As long as it had a door I felt like I had made it to the big league. On the first morning in my new digs, I opened the door to find what looked like a completely new office. The desk was sparkling, the conference table looked new, the chairs all matched and the broken file cabinet had been removed. The entire day everyone who walked by congratulated me on my promotion and asked how in the world I got my office in such shape. I had no idea. Maybe the maintenance guys realized someone was moving in and cleaned everything up? No way, everyone highly doubted it.

Then 5 p.m. came around and Maria stopped by to collect my trash. She had this proud grin on her face and said, "Te gusta?" So Maria was behind it! I got up to thank her profusely. I couldn't believe she had gone through such trouble. "De nada. De nada. Un placer," she said and then proceeded to explain that it was the least she could do after everything I had done for her. *Everything I had done for her? What would that be?* I started to wonder if she mistook me for another person but no, she was referring to the fact that I would take time to say hello everyday when she came to clean my work space. It turned out that this gesture alone made all the difference when everyone else rushed past her or didn't say word. "Before you moved to this floor I could have been invisible," she explained. "Now I enjoy coming to work." It was one of the first times in my adult life when I felt like I was turning into my mother. And it was a good feeling.

Another "mom moment" was at my wedding, the planning of which my mother and I sweetly indulged in (with regular input from the groom, of course). Weddings have tested mother-daughter relationships throughout time but in my case I don't know what I would have done without mine. For as long as I can remember my mother and I had been saving magazine clippings of ideas we'd one day want to incorporate into my wedding. When the day came for us to start planning an actual wedding vs. a theoretical one, we were beyond prepared. Even before we were officially engaged, Alex and I talked about getting married in the Philippines. It held

Walking down the aisle (2009)

a special place for us ever since he visited me there and during the trip he often commented on how he wished his family could experience everything he was seeing. Our wedding a couple years down the line turned out to be the perfect opportunity.

Our wedding would also be the first time Alex saw my mother's lifelong relationships in full effect. Starting with her siblings and extending to her childhood friends it seemed everyone on my mother's Top 100 had a part to play in the wedding planning:

- Her sister, Tita Lynn, has a restaurant catering business so she and her staff took care of the entire menu for the week-long string of events from welcome reception to rehearsal dinner to wedding reception to post wedding brunch to country side lunch, etc.
- Her oldest brother, Tito Armand, is a member of the most

exclusive clubs and he always offered to host us at Manila Golf or Manila Polo.

- Her youngest brother, Tito Francis, is an attorney who took care of all the paperwork we needed including countless permits and licenses from the city and church.
- Her close friend Rachy Cuna is a famous designer and renowned floral architect who often partnered with Tita Lynn on major events, and he offered to take care of our wedding decor and flowers.
- Another close friend, Tito Raul (who also happens to be the first cousin of Tita Lynn's husband Tito Rene), is a world renowned concert pianist and he arranged for the University of Santo Tomas choir to perform all the music for the church ceremony.
- Her aunt, Tita Elma, has a personal connection with actor-singer John Arcilla and she arranged for him to do a solo performance of "The Prayer" as a prelude to the Mass.
- Her nephew Jon Jon and his wife, Karen, had their own event planning business, and they helped coordinate everything from the wedding cake to the gift bags.
- Her second cousin, Tita Cris, worked for Japan Airlines and helped us arrange for 40 of our friends to fly over to the Philippines together from New York ("the party plane" it was later called).
- Her college friends, Tito Titus and Tita Bochie, are in the music business so they took us around town to listen to different bands and then negotiated on our behalf with the manager of Freestyle.
- Another group of college friends, the CAFA Singers, sang my parents' wedding song, "Sunrise, Sunset" as a surprise for me.
- Another friend, Tita Ching, has a sister who is a travel agent and when she caught wind of a deal on Cebu Pacific that required tickets to be purchased in person she had her son line up for hours to secure the flights to Boracay for all our wedding guests.

Party plane to Boracay (2009)

- Her second (or third) cousin, Tito Jerry, had access to several vans so he arranged shuttle transportation to and from all the hotels where our guests were staying.
- One of her closest friends, Tita Cecile, volunteered to go to the local shopping markets and buy sarongs and flip flops that would go into the gift bags she purchased on our behalf. She asked us for all the names of our female guests and personalized each tote bag using a special textured paint.
- Another friend of the family, Tita Emma, is the food and beverage manager at Sea Wind Resort in Boracay and she arranged accommodations for all our guests after our wedding in Manila.

The list of happy helpers went on and on. At one point during our wedding reception while guests were dining on the main course and Alex and I were taking in everything, he looked at me and said, "Only you could get a hundred people to travel across the world to the Philippines during a global economic crisis.[73] Well, only you and your mother... ." I looked around the room and saw the faces of the most important people at every stage of my life. Childhood friends and JAM 4 HELP co-founders from Vancouver, the popular girls from UNIS who eventually ended up becoming my best friends, the go getter Yalies who turned out to be like big brothers and little sisters, friends I made during six-month stints around the world and friends I made doing projects to promote the Philippines. Somehow my relationships with each of them had become lifelong. Maybe I did pick up a thing or two from my mother.

Justin, Mom and Tita Tessie
(2009)

I do hope to have more "mom moments" especially as my children grow up. They make me feel mindful and grounded. Like I'm not forgetting where I came from. Like I'm not forgetting the soap. I never used to understand what my parents meant when they would say, "It would be easier for us to give you what you want, but making you wait is actually for you... ." Now I think of it every time Carlos asks for "Toby" (one of the Thomas and Friends trains) and we tell him he'll need to wait for his birthday (nine months away) even if the toy is already sitting in my bedside drawer.

The other day as we were packing up and moving apartments, Carlos came by and placed a Kit Kat bar on top of one of the boxes. "I'm sharing this with the kids who

---

[73] It was just a few months after the fall of Bear Stearns and Lehman Brothers.

Lola Lenore and her two grandchildren

don't have chocolate." I am not sure what made me happier—that he gets the concept of giving or that he was putting his share in the *balikbayan* box.

As I come to the end of the book there are a few things I want to acknowledge.

1. I learned just as much from my father as I did from my mother; he's just not as vocal. Instead of saying, "Maybe you shouldn't wear that lipstick," he'll make me wear an ugly hot pink flourescent cap. One of my mother's reminders is actually to take a lesson from my father. She often tells him that he needs to write a book about confidence because he never gets intimidated or embarrassed. This quality has served them very well. In fact, my parents may have never made it past their immigration interview if not for my father's audacity, but that's a story for the next book.

2. I know my mother's not perfect despite this book homage. I remember the first time I realized she had flaws. We were at a Pizza Hut in Coquitlam with a big group of family friends and my mother saw Justin and me taking green peppers off our slices. "Don't remove the vegetables," she instructed, "They're good for you and that's wasteful." We obeyed as usual and forced ourselves to eat all the undesired toppings. Minutes later Justin tapped me and pointed at my mother. She was removing the green peppers, the mushrooms and the onions. "*Mom,*" we called out, "why aren't *you* eating your vegetables?" It was the first (and maybe only) time I've seen her look guilty.

In general my mother's food habits leave room for improvement. It's not like she gorges herself on junk food or eats late at night or anything but her diet is straight out of the 1950s and hasn't changed much since. One of her favorite dishes to serve is corned beef dip (she has since renamed "Friendship Dip"). The recipe consists of one can of Campbell's Cream of Mushroom soup, one block of Philadelphia Cream Cheese, one cup of Hellman's Mayonnaise, and one can of Libby's Corned Beef (I recently learned the original recipe called for crab meat but the Filipino moms replaced it with corned beef since it was cheaper).

My mother picked up this recipe over two decades ago when we were growing up in Vancouver where it had become a staple dish at all of our gatherings. She continued serving the corned beef dip at all our parties in New York. When our childhood friends saw it on Facebook recently they were flabbergasted. For them it was a mere memory – something we all used to eat before we learned better. For our family it was something we still made for gatherings once, maybe twice, a month. Exchanging messages about the dip and the good old days did make everyone nostalgic, however, and this past Christmas we all agreed to serve it at our respective dinner parties.

The corned beef dip turned out to be a hit at everyone's holiday gathering (no surprise to Justin and me). You can turn your nose up all you want at the ingredients but we know it's always a winner. That said, it is admittedly the opposite of wholesome and apparently all our family friends started adjusting their diet faster than we did. In retrospect, Justin and I did start noticing on trips back to Vancouver that our friends' moms have started serving brown rice instead of white, replaced fatty pork with lean chicken, and given more prominence to salads on dinner tables. It seemed we were the only ones whose food regimen didn't change with the times.

Family photo (2012)

3. If you found yourself rolling your eyes as you read any part of this book, that's OK. My husband tried to help me "decornify" a few sections for the general non-sitcom audience, but I don't expect it to have worked entirely.

One last reminder (for now). Use the good stuff. My mother often tells us that we should make a point to use nice things on ourselves, and not just save them for special guests or occasions. "Who, after all, could be more special than my family?" she exclaims. She had fun teaching us this lesson one day when she and my father were preparing all afternoon for a fancy dinner while Justin and I kept trying to guess who the guests might be. My mother had set aside the fine china for which she had spent years saving and my father had pulled out of the linen cabinet our elegant hand embroidered tablecloth and napkins. Every time we would ask "Who's our special guest?" my mother would respond, "The most important people in the world."

"The Pope? Cory Aquino? Queen Elizabeth?" That was about as important as you could get in our Filipino-Canadian household.

My parents kept us guessing until it was time to answer the doorbell. Justin and I ran to the front door (the one only used by special guests, Jehovah's Witnesses and door-to-door salesmen since most of our friends would just come up the patio stairs that led directly to our kitchen). It seemed no one was there so we kept peering out to the side until we turned around to find our parents greeting us.

"Welcome, welcome! Come on in," they chimed as they directed us to the sitting room. We followed them back into the house and sat on our fancy chairs still a little confused.

"We have a very special dinner planned for you since you're so important to us." Ah, I finally got it.

"Why, thank you! It was a long trip but it's nice to be here." I played along.

After a little more chitchat we sat down in the dining room and saw all our fine things laid out beautifully on the table alongside a delicious looking spread: Spaghetti Bolognese (of course, we didn't call it "Bolognese" back then), Nana Flor's homemade dinner rolls, Black Forest Chocolate Cake from Safeway, and Filipino fruit salad with Nestlé cream (these two desserts defined our childhood).

I was enjoying this family dinner party and loving the idea of using the good stuff on ourselves when halfway through his plate Justin looked up and asked our parents, "But wait, what are the special guests going to eat?"

You could almost hear the laugh track.

Waiting at the altar (2009)

First dance (2009)

Bridesmaids
(2009)

Line dancing (2009)

Photo with all our relatives (2009)

Wedding reception (2009)

Ang Kasal (The Wedding) Reunion in NYC. From left to right: Marcel, May, me, J Ray, Bianca, Alexis, Faisal, Steph (2009)

Some of our closest friends. Top left to right: Danny, Sheldon. Middle left to right: Bianca, Yara, Carissa, J Ray, Tina. Bottom left to right: Kristen, Katja, James, me, Gaurav, Julianna (2009)

Dad with some of my closest girlfriend (the stern Asian man no longer). From left to right: May, Tanya, Alexis, Olivia and Bianca (2009)

Taking Carlos to visit the family ancestral home in Taal, Batangas (2013)

Group shot at Luneta Park. One of my proudest achievements—bringing tourism to the Philippines! (2009)

Author Bio

Marie Claire Lim Moore
(October 30, 1976) is a Filipina-
Canadian-American working
mother and author of *Don't
Forget the Soap*. After spending
the early part of her childhood
in Vancouver, Claire moved
to New York City and attended the United Nations
International School. She went on to study at Yale,
climb the corporate ladder at Citi and travel around the
world. She met her husband, Alex, while working in Sao
Paulo, Brazil and they married in Manila, Philippines
shortly before moving to Singapore. Now Mom to
Carlos and Isabel, Claire also manages the Global Client
business for Citi in Asia. She enjoys juggling career
and family and likes to throw in community and politics
for fun by campaigning for US political candidates,
fund-raising for organizations that advance the role
of women in business and promoting foreign direct
investment in the Philippines. She is also a guest
contributor at *Sassy Mama Singapore*.

71037004R00136

Made in the USA
San Bernardino, CA
10 March 2018